ANALYSING ARCHITECTI

A rchitecture is such a rich and subtle field of human creativity that it is impossible to encapsulate it completely in a single book. I tried to describe some of the basics in an earlier book, *Analysing Architecture*, which has now appeared in four editions, increasing in size each time. But even though that book has almost doubled in content, there is more to cover. So, rather than make the original even heavier, I have decided to add further chapters as a series of separate smaller volumes.

These *Analysing Architecture Notebooks* are the new chapters I would have added to *Analysing Architecture* had not excessive size become a concern. The series format also allows me to explore topics at greater length than if I were confined to just a few extra pages in the original book. Nevertheless the shared aim remains the same: to explore and expose the workings of architecture in ways that might help those who face the challenges of doing it.

Simon Unwin is Emeritus Professor of Architecture at the University of Dundee in Scotland. Although retired, he continues to teach at the Welsh School of Architecture in Cardiff University, Wales, where he taught for many years. His books are used in schools of architecture around the world and have been translated into various languages.

Books by Simon Unwin

Analysing Architecture
An Architecture Notebook: Wall
Doorway
Exercises in Architecture – Learning to Think as an Architect
Twenty-Five Buildings Every Architect Should Understand
The Ten Most Influential Buildings in History: Architecture's Archetypes

ebooks (available from the iBooks Store)

Skara Brae
The Entrance Notebook
Villa Le Lac
The Time Notebook

The Analysing Architecture Notebook Series

Metaphor
Curve
Children as Place-Makers

Simon Unwin's website is at *simonunwin.com*

Some of Simon Unwin's personal notebooks, used in researching and preparing this
and his other books, are available for free download from his website.

ANALYSING ARCHITECTURE NOTEBOOKS

CHILDREN

AS PLACE-MAKERS

the innate architect in all of us

First published 2019
by Routledge
2 Park Square, Milton Park, Abingdon, Oxon OX14 4RN

and by Routledge
52 Vanderbilt Avenue, New York, NY 10017

Routledge is an imprint of the Taylor & Francis Group, an informa business

Publisher's Note
This book has been prepared from camera-ready copy provided by the author.

British Library Cataloguing-in-Publication Data
A catalogue record for this book is available from the British Library

Library of Congress Cataloging-in-Publication Data
Names: Unwin, Simon, 1952- author.
Title: Children as place-makers : the innate architect in all of us / Simon Unwin.
Description: New York : Routledge, 2019. | Series: The analysing architecture notebook series | Includes bibliographical references and index.
Identifiers: LCCN 2018058225| ISBN 9781138046009 (hb : alk. paper) | ISBN 9781138046016 (pb : alk. paper) | ISBN 9781315171623 (ebook)
Subjects: LCSH: Architecture--Human factors.
Classification: LCC NA2542.4 .U57 2019 | DDC 720.1/03--dc23
LC record available at https://lccn.loc.gov/2018058225

ISBN: 978-1-138-04600-9 (hbk)
ISBN: 978-1-138-04601-6 (pbk)
ISBN: 978-1-315-17162-3 (ebk)

Typeset in Arial and Georgia

by Simon Unwin

for Idris bach

We are all architects of our own worlds. This is evident in our childhood selves: when we make dens in woods and caves, camps and sandcastles on the beach, make-believe fortresses on rocky cliffs, houses in trees and under tables…
Architecture – place-making – is a language to itself. We all have a subconscious fluency in that language, and an innate capacity for it that can be developed with practice. But for many of us that capacity has been consigned to subliminal dormancy by the dominating focus in school on words and numbers.
Nevertheless, the innate architect is in us all.

CONTENTS

PREFACE 1

INTRODUCTION: THE VERBS OF ARCHITECTURE 7

RELATING TO THE WORLD 23

PLACE CREATION 53

MAKING PLACES WITH OURSELVES 83

DEFINING PLACE 91

PLACES FOR GAMES 105

CIRCLE 109

BOX 147

BUILDING PLACES 151

PLACES OF THE IMAGINATION 165

ENDNOTE 173

ACKNOWLEDGEMENTS 176

BIBLIOGRAPHY 177

INDEX 180

'... we children
were construction workers,
clearing glades in the woods for dens,
tree-houses, bird-hides, lookouts.
We'd ease into hollow trees
and whisper in the mushroomy dark.'

Gillian Clarke – 'Letting the Light In', in *Recipe for Water*, 2009.

'We are all storytellers. We make stories to make sense of our lives.'

Stephen Grosz – *The Examined Life: How We Lose and Find Ourselves*, 2013.

PREFACE

Often, in adult discourse, children are referred to in the third person – as 'they' or 'them' – as if they were a distinct species; as if at some point in our development we cross a definitive divide between childhood and adulthood. That distinction does not apply here. As far as this Notebook is concerned, we all retain some potential for freshness and directness in our relationship with the physical world around us throughout our lives; I mean when we act intuitively to create rudimentary places using only our own bodies or simple readily available resources. This potential is evident in the relaxed place-making we engage in when, for example, we spend a day on the beach, as well as in the less relaxed place-making imposed on some of us by indigence and homelessness.

In this Notebook I have sought to illustrate the innate architect in all of us by looking primarily at the places we make when we are young, when architecture is, or is close to being, intuitive; when architecture seems to emerge as a 'mother' or even natural language of spatial relationship with our surroundings.

At all stages of life we are inescapably in dialogue with our physical surroundings. We adopt places we find. We propose and create new places when we feel the desire or when the need arises. We express meaning about our relationship with the world by occupying and amending it. It is through place-making that we make sense of where we find ourselves.

Though as replete with the potential for meaning and the proposition of ideas as our mother tongue, architecture is not a verbal language (even though, very occasionally, it might employ a few words). Architecture is generally a 'silent', almost subliminal, language of place identification and spatial organisation. Its elements are markers, lines defining thresholds and areas of ground, walls, pathways...

As we develop from babies into young children we learn, gradually, how to use verbal language. Such development attracts huge general and academic interest. Parents are understandably excited when their child utters his or her first word, divining 'mama' or 'papa' from the earliest indistinct babbling. Educationalists go around in large circles discussing how language (and reading skills) should be developed in school. What attracts less general interest (seemingly because it is 'silent' and subliminal), but which is no less exciting and consequential, is our development of an understanding of space, how we situate ourselves in our surroundings and how we manipulate them to our own desires and needs; i.e. how we learn, at its most rudimentary level and both as users and makers, architecture.

Before we are born we occupy one of the principal, if not the most important, models for (and metaphors evident in*) architecture – the womb. After we emerge into the world we have places of comfort and protection provided for us: a parent's arms; the blankets of a cradle or cot; the buggy or pram; the incarceration of a high chair and playpen; the home itself... But as we grow and become more mobile we begin to make our own places. We do this first by recognition, trial and adoption: we might sit on a cushion or tuffet; crawl behind a sofa or under a table; walk holding hands along the top of a wall. Gradually we realise that we are ourselves active agents in the world, we can change it according to our own whims, our needs and desires: maybe we gather our toy friends in a tight circle about us or make a nest of cushions; maybe we draw a circle in the sand and sit in it; maybe we build a house of cardboard boxes; maybe we hang blankets on the table to enclose the space beneath and enjoy the experience of dark envelopment it provides.

As children we deal with the world intuitively but we also learn from what we experience. These processes work in our acquisition of language; they work in our acquisition of architecture too. But whereas language is culturally and nationally specific, it seems that the rudiments of architecture are universal, common to all people (and animals too). At its rudimentary level, architecture is a corollary of being in the world. With regard to language we can be silent; but with

---

* See *Metaphor*, also in this Analysing Architecture Notebook series, pages 6–7.

regard to architecture we cannot be not somewhere – we are always in and interacting with place; and place is the seed of all architecture.

Some of the fundamental conceptual structures of architecture will become evident in the pages of this Notebook. Whether they are intuitive or learnt is not of primary concern here. My aim has been more to explore how the rudiments of architecture – all architecture, including the most sophisticated works produced by professional architects – are evident in those ephemeral, deceptively simple yet engagingly subtle places we make as children.

In his detailed study of *Children's Experience of Place* (1979), Roger Hart observed that often children took more pleasure in the construction of dens (forts) than in their use; i.e. that the experience and challenges of *making* were of more value to the children than *having*. This seems to be another way in which architecture can be compared to verbal language. For when children use language the experience of forming sentences and achieving communication is of more value than the 'possession' of a sentence. Language is a forum of active creation. It is the same with architecture: the fun lies primarily in the present action of making a place rather than in having the result. Often the places we make as children are ephemeral: soon, if not immediately, to be wiped away either by ourselves or by the tide.

*'Damn braces: Bless relaxes.' *

The subject of this Notebook might be termed 'play architecture' except that to do so might be inferred by the reader as suggesting that the places we make 'as children' should not be taken particularly seriously because they are 'merely' ephemeral. (One might observe that all uttered sentences are 'merely ephemeral' too! But we take them seriously.) In analysing the places we make as children, we find, as we might reasonably expect, that we are revealing the fundamental language of place identification and spatial organisation that underpins all architecture, whatever level of sophistication it might attain.

Even so, play, imagination, story-telling... as well as intuitive psychological responses to the world in which we find ourselves, are all evident in the ephemeral places we make as children. Without the benefits

---

* William Blake – *The Marriage of Heaven and Hell* (1793), 1976.

(and restraints) of experience and instruction, as children we make places unselfconsciously but not without engaging our imaginations. The rudimentary places we make can be subtle and sophisticated, they can transport us across the seas to magical lands. By studying examples we can become more aware of what we feel is important to us – our aspirations – when we seek to make a place. By studying rudimentary examples we can gain a greater understanding of the powers underlying more sophisticated and permanent architecture – powers that can change our perception of our surroundings and our sense of ourselves. The places we make as children are replete with wordless poetry. They speak, tacitly and in direct terms, of our relationships with the world and with each other. We respond to them intuitively, recognising the profound manifestation of the human condition they represent.

In the following passage from a paper published in the 1980s, environmental psychologists Maxine Wolfe and Leanne Rivlin hint at the ways rudimentary architecture – in particular the ways children may be required to adhere to an authoritan regime of 'lining up' – can restrict children's free personal expression in the cause of control:

'One of the clearest, yet most unquestioned, examples of an institutional routine designed to provide structure is "lining up". It is rationalized as a necessary component of the ongoing program, as a method of making non-functional transition time as efficient as possible. In psychiatric facilities, children line up before and after every activity. After they wake up, they line up for showering; then they line up to go to the dining room for breakfast. They line up in the dining room to obtain their food, and they line up after eating to go back to their living areas. After a short while, they line up to go to their first activities of the day. In schools, students line up in the yard or basement before going to their classes; they line up within their classrooms even when they are going a short distance down the hall. They line up before and after lunch to go to the cafeteria and to the school yard and to re-enter the school. In most lining-up situations children are expected to behave in a totally self-controlled manner even when they are compacted into a small space within a group. Children are required to remain lined up behaving appropriately for as long as it takes for this to be done properly by all involved.' *

---

* Maxine Wolfe and Leanne G. Rivlin – 'Institutions in Children's Lives', in Weinstein and David – *Spaces for Children*, 1987, p. 103.

Since architecture is about spatial organisation, 'lining up' is a rudimentary example of architecture, an example in which architecture may be imposed on children. Much of the architecture we experience is similarly, if benevolently, controlling. Its sets the spatial frame – the spatial rule systems – within which we live. It sets down for us where we can walk, which space is ours, which belongs to someone else, where we can (are allowed to) engage in particular activities, and so on.

Undoubtedly, in many circumstances, the spatial control exercised by architecture is beneficial for the general good. The example of 'lining up' described in the above quotation is imposed by authority for the purpose of efficient management of a situation. And the organised layout of houses and cities – designed by professional architects acting under the restraints of political (planning) authority – mitigates what might otherwise be spatial anarchy. But the places we make as children (i.e. all of us when we behave as children) are free of such authority. They express our intuitive, direct, unselfconscious relationships with space and with each other. Architectural activity on the beach, around the house, in the woods or the playground... – the untrammelled recognition and identification of place – is a realm of free personal expression for all of us. It derives from an innate instinct for architecture. Through it we develop our capacity to make places for ourselves. This realm is the primordial intellectual χώρα – 'chora' (to use Plato's word, which is often translated as 'receptacle of becoming') – from which all architecture develops.

The physical space around us is not something we merely occupy. It is something with which we have a symbiotic relationship: space accommodates us and we mould space to our purposes. We may not be able to change the progress of time – only measure it and organise our own schedules – but our relationship with space is both inter- and pro-active: we can manipulate, amend, change, organise it. It is this capacity that makes us all architects. From childhood through adulthood, as the following pages will show, the innate architect is in us all.

Architecture is a non-verbal mode of communication – a language (generally) without words by which we make sense of the space of the world in which we live. In the following examples, I have tried to interpret and translate, from the architectural to the verbal, what in each example the child architect is 'saying' through their place-making.

But the primary expression – the one the reader should relate to and empathise with – is that presented architecturally. For the most part I shall leave you to draw parallels between the places we make as children and more permanent architecture (though occasionally in the following pages I have made some comparisons). But the evidence is clear that architecture is a common language – shared by all human beings as well as some other creatures – which informs all its products, from the rudimentary to the sophisticated.

My abiding interest, throughout my career as a teacher of architecture, has been how to help students learn to become architects; i.e. I have sought to explore how architecture works and how it might be done. The vast majority of early-years students, when they begin, find it difficult. It seems that after years of formal education pursued primarily through the media of verbal language and mathematics, they have lost contact with the reference framework by which to understand how to engage with the activity of architecture – which is, at its essence, neither verbal nor mathematical. One of the purposes of this Notebook is to demonstrate to such students that, rather than being some strange impenetrable field of creativity, architecture is a language the rudiments of which they already know, if only unconsciously.

To get started, all you need to do is to reawaken the dormant child architect inside yourself.

You can colour in the pictures if you wish!

'The motivation to interact with the environment exists in all children as an intrinsic property of life.'

Anita Rui Olds, quoted in Carol Simon Weinstein – 'Designing Preschool Classrooms to Support Development', in Weinstein and David – *Spaces for Children*, 1987, p. 181.

'I am the King. I tell. I am not told. I am the verb, sir. I am not the object.'

Alan Bennett – *The Madness of George III*, 1992.

INTRODUCTION
THE VERBS OF ARCHITECTURE

Architecture is a doing word; it is action before product. And the key agent of action is the person, the child, the architect. Though architecture is often thought of as consisting of achieved buildings – houses, churches, opera houses... – for the architect in us it is different: it is the process of conceiving and realising... having ideas and making them real.

In *Analysing Architecture* (4th edition, 2014, page 28) I suggested that place is to architecture as meaning is to language. Meaning is the essential burden of language; place is the essential burden of architecture. Like language, architecture has its grammar – its parts and patterns of structure. Like language architecture has its verbs: the 'doings' that contribute to place-making. This section illustrates some of the key verbs of architecture. They drive permanent and sophisticated architecture but they are evident too in the rudimentary place-making we engage in as children.

(Subtle variations on the verbs of architecture will become evident throughout this Notebook. These are listed in the 'I...' entries in the Index.)

TO BE
I am

I am. And, in being, I am both the subject and origin of architecture.

Architecture is in me and is generated from me. Architecture is a corollary of my presence. In itself my form brings architecture into the world. I identify my place. I project architecture – direction and order – around me.

The world is given its four directions – its 'four corners' – by my presence. Upright, my axis extends infinitely up into the sky and down into the ground. The surface of the earth is my base and territory.

My presence is apparent from as far away as I can be seen. I stand as a marker of my own circle of existence. I am the centre of my world.

Architecture is in my image. 'To be' is the fundamental architectural verb.

I identify a place.
You identify a place.
He, she, it identifies a place.

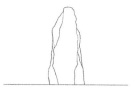

An upright stone stands as a vicarious representative of its architect.

TO LIVE
I live

I live; I am alive. I generate an aura of vitality.

In time, my heart beats. I breathe. My eyes observe and engage. I smile. I project my vitality into the world around me.

I wave my arms, I kick my legs, I dance, I play…

I laugh. I cry. I shout and sing.

I dream, I imagine, I pretend…

I am happy, sad, angry, scared…

I act…

Living, I occupy space; more than merely that space bounded by the outer surface of my body. My place is inflated about me by my vitality, like a bubble.

'To live' is more than 'to be'. As a verb 'to live' multiplies the dimensions of architecture many fold.

I breathe, I see, I dance…
I laugh and cry and sing…

An inert body generates architecture… But living, more is brought into play.

TO MOVE
I crawl, walk, run...

I crawl, I walk, I run. I reach. I move from here to there, and there; and back again. I explore. I discover... Exploring, I draw invisible dynamic lines – pathways. And by these pathways I map my world with an ever-growing route-map.

To map is to make sense. To move from place to place, to create a network of pathways, is to give the world an architecture of sense by which I understand it and give it form in my mind. By this map I know where I am... unless I get lost; in which case my world dissolves, my architecture fails.

' "What do you do, exactly?"...
"I reify... It's a serious job."
"I see... Serious work, with big books and a big table cluttered with papers."
"No... I walk. Mostly I walk." '

I explore my world by crawling, walking, running around. In doing so I map it; I give it architecture.

Lines of movement are made permanent by paved pathways.

Michèle Bernstein, trans. Kelsey – *All the King's Horses* (1960), 2008.

TO CROSS A THRESHOLD
I cross lines

I encounter lines that cross my pathways – thresholds, transitions between places of different character: wet and dry; light and dark; warm and cold; safe and dangerous... Sometimes I hesitate, but I try crossing them. There is a thrill in crossing them. There is risk and anticipation in crossing thresholds.

I learn what happens when I cross a threshold. Sometimes bad things happen – I get wet or fall, I might get scolded. But sometimes I am rewarded – I find myself somewhere I enjoy being. I learn about thresholds: when to cross them; when not to; when to take care.

I include thresholds in my map of the world. They punctuate my pathways. Thresholds are elements in the architecture by which I make sense of the world.

I can cross thresholds. Sometimes I discover the error of doing so.

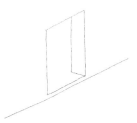

Our experience of the world is punctuated by thresholds.

TO OWN
I own (my space)

I occupy space actively. By occupying a place, I give it identity. It belongs to me.

While I am here, I own this place. It is my place, even if only for a short time. Wherever I am, I invest a place with my identity.

My possession of this place may be ephemeral or I may settle here for some time. It may be threatened by tide or challenge. But while I occupy it, it is mine.

Maybe I leave an impression. My identification – ownership – of the place lingers even when I have gone (until erased by tide, wind or other people).

Sometimes I wish I could define my place more clearly, more tangibly, more permanently… make it more secure. Perhaps I want to *establish* my place in the world, actually and metaphorically.

I establish a place, if only for a moment, by occupying it. It is my place. It is where I am.

We leave traces of our presence, impressions in the sand…

TO DEFINE
I draw a boundary (about my place)

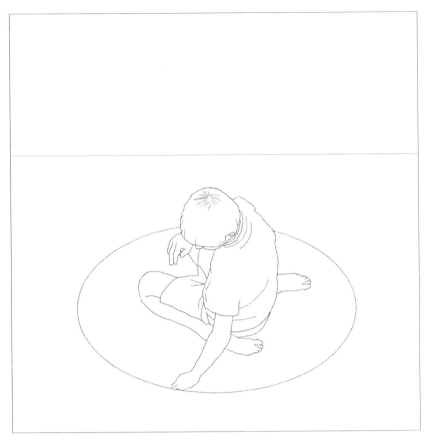

I can define my place by drawing boundaries. I draw a plan of my place, full scale, on the ground around me. By doing so it becomes clear, precise. I give architectural form to my bubble of space. By drawing this circle I define my own threshold, my own horizon – delimit the circular mini-world I claim and know as mine, over which I hold sway. I draw a line at which others might hesitate. I generate a psychological carapace within which I feel more secure, stronger. The defining line on the ground establishes my place. This circle defines my home. I can leave it and come back to it. By reference to it I know where I am. In it my identity persists even when I am not there.

The definitive case consolidates and perpetuates the possessive.

I can define my place with the reach of my arm, drawing a circle around myself.

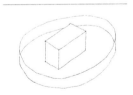

Houses, churches, temples… sit in defined areas of ground.

TO MARK
I mark (a spot)

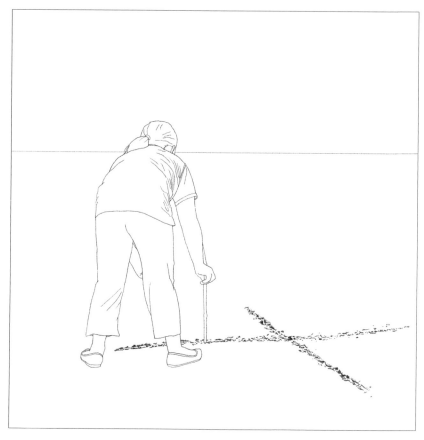

Place is where the mind touches the world. Even in featureless terrain, I can select an unmarked location and make it particular even though no one else can see it. Merely by selection I can identify a place. In itself that is an architectural act.

But then I can mark that location – maybe by planting a stick or by drawing a cross on the ground – and straight away that particular spot is distinguished from everywhere else architecturally, in a way that others can see. That spot is given tangible identity. It becomes a place that can be seen as such.

I can identify a place by erecting a marker visible from afar (below). This is an act of architecture.

'The marking of ground, rather than the primitive hut, is the primordial tectonic act.'

Vittorio Gregotti – 'Address to the Architectural League, New York, 1982', 1983.

TO POINT
I point at (something over there)

I could identify that location just by pointing at it. By lines of sight and by pointing, I can project my perception and understanding of the world outwards. I can draw attention. By pointing I communicate what I see and want to indicate to others.

My sight and pointing establish linkage between me, my place, and objects and places that are remote from me. I might point at that unmarked spot to make it apparent. I might point at something I want or see as a threat. I might point to where I want to go.

Pointing is architectural. In my image, works of architecture can point too. By doing so they establish linkage with the remote.

Just by seeing I establish a link between me and a distant object. By pointing I make that link stronger.

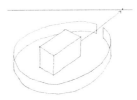

By their geometry and openings buildings too can point at remote objects.

TO RECOGNISE
I see (somewhere as a place)

I recognise a potential place when I see it. By doing so I convert it, mentally, into a place.

Recognising features and their potential as places is part of how I make sense of the world around me. I see a rock that could serve as a seat, a ledge that could be a shelf, a cave in which I could hide, a tree under which I might sit...

By recognising a feature as a potential place, I transform it into architecture (defined as identification of place). And I can share that sense, that architecture, with others. I can say, 'Look! There's a rock'; or, 'Let's sit under that tree'. The rock becomes a seat. The tree becomes a house. This is not just imagination at work.

Architecture, even when no more than a matter of my mind's recognition and selection of places, alters my world.

I recognise features around me as places.

I recognise a tree, a rock and a cave as places that I might occupy.

ANALYSING ARCHITECTURE NOTEBOOKS

TO OCCUPY
I occupy, inhabit (a place)

I move towards a place I recognise as such. I enter it. I occupy it. I sit on the rock or under the tree. I hide in the cave. I inhabit it. Now the recognised place becomes the locus of my personal bubble.

There is a mutual relationship between me and the place. I discover it. It accommodates me. I possess it. I lend it my identity. My presence, my bubble, expands (or contracts) to fill the place – the space under the tree canopy, the space within the cave. (The sitting rock's space is less clearly defined). Inhabitation is the apotheosis of a place. When I occupy a cave or sit under a tree I fill it with my vitality.

The tree and the cave become architecture by reason of my occupation of their space, by my inhabitation of that space as place.

I recognise a rock as a place to sit… and then sit upon it.

We might sit under the tree or in the cave. They become 'houses'.

TO PUT
I put (something where I think it should be)

I put a toy on a table; a wooden brick on top of another; a crayon in a jar... I *place* them.

I recognise places around me but I do not always occupy them myself. Sometimes I put something else in a place.

As when selecting a place for myself, I weigh up the possibilities of the places I recognise. I try to sit teddy on a rock, but perhaps he falls off. I learn what works and what does not. The crayon placed in a jar stays there, where I can find it.

The situation is transactional. I learn to analyse the characteristics of places I recognise and judge whether they suit my purpose or offer possibilities I had not foreseen.

Placing – siting – is essential to architecture at rudimentary and sophisticated levels.

I can sit my teddy on a rock, like a king on a throne.

Teddy could be a temple, a church or a fortress... sitting on a high crag.

TO HIDE
I hide (myself from others or from some threat)

I can hide things – place them out of sight – but sometimes I hide myself.

I am able to recognise places where I could disappear from general sight.

Hiding is fun. It provokes puzzlement and concern in those who cannot find me. It causes laughter of surprise and relief when I am discovered or when I leap out of my hiding place suddenly, scream-laughing.

Hiding is a survival skill too. I might need to hide from threats. Practising is preparation. Hiding from the world gives me psychological comfort, some privacy, some time with my own thoughts. We hide from the world in our houses.

Architecture can be about identifying (finding or making) a place in which to hide.

I can find a place to hide, even if not quite successfully.

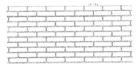

We build walls as screens, behind which we can hide from the world.

TO MODIFY
I alter (somewhere to make it a place)

I can modify a place to make it suit my purpose better.

Locations I recognise as potential places might not be quite how I want them. They need some modification. I might brush away ants, or wipe away drops of water… Finding a place in sand dunes from which to survey the sea I might scoop out some sand to make it into a comfortable seat.

To play cricket, or perform some other ritual, I might clear an area of ground of stones and litter. Maybe I would need to fill in holes too. The place I make will be defined by its smoothness, and by the line of discarded stones and litter around its boundary.

Place-making need be no more than a matter of modification, a matter of clearing ground.

I find a place in the dunes from which to watch the sea. By scooping out a few handfuls of sand I make a seat (or throne).

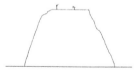

Some peoples in ancient times levelled the tops of peaks as sanctuaries.

TO SIGN
I sign (a place with my name, initials, logo...)

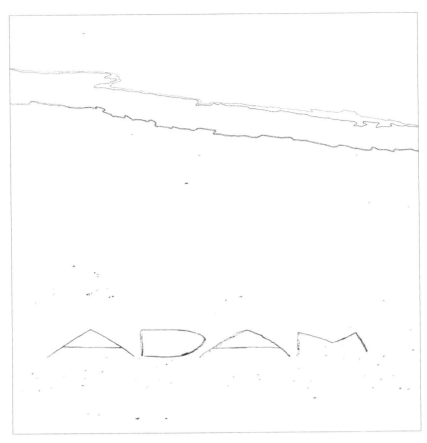

I can give identity to a place by signing it.

Signing and its relationship with place can take many forms. Signing might involve drawing a picture or symbol on the wall of a deep cave. Leaving a footprint in soft earth, as forensic detectives exploit, can be a way of determining that a suspected miscreant visited a particular place. Footprints petrified in mud have been found dating back many thousands of years.

If I write my name in the sand, the incoming tide will wash it away in a few hours. If I carve my initials in the trunk of a tree, the record of my presence might last many years – until the bark grows over or the tree itself dies and rots away. If I leave my mark engraved in the rock wall of a cave, my association with that place might last for millennia (and puzzle archaeologists).

I want others to know that I am or have been here, in this place.

Inscriptions may carry various messages, but primarily one of presence.

TO MAKE
I dig and construct (new places)

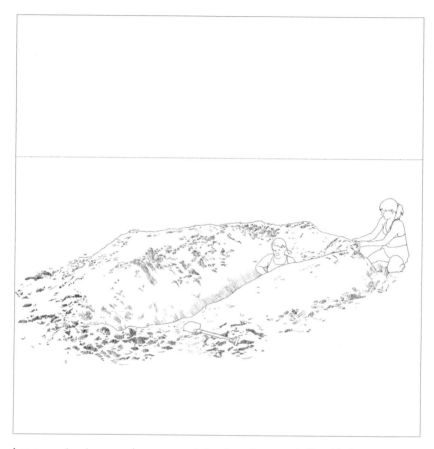

I can construct a new place on a pristine beach.

I might modify a place I recognise to suit my purpose better (page 20). But I can conjure up new places from nowhere too. I can build places that did not previously exist, in locations where there are no features to recognise or change.

On a beach the sand is my material. I dig pits and mound walls. I can excavate holes in which to sit. I can build walls with rocks ready to hand, driftwood, plants, or just sand... I can construct a house or a shrine, a refuge or a fort...

In conceiving places I am an architect. In constructing them I am a builder too.

In the wide featureless expanse of a beach smoothed by the receding tide, with a little effort I can conjure up a walled pit for my sister to sit inside. As an architect, I have created a place that did not previously exist. I have, in my small (but nevertheless profound) way, changed the world.

All these verbs play their part in our lives as architects. The following pages explore how they play out in the places we make as children. In those pages you will also see these verbs have subtle variations.*

 * See Index entries under 'I…'.

'If a child acquires the knowledge and understanding of who it is by virtue of its dependent and continuing relationships to significant other people, then we must assume that such identity determinations are also rooted in the child's experience with rooms, clothes, playthings, and an entire range of objects and spaces that also support its existence. Certainly this inanimate world is ever present and inherent in the child's interactions and relationships with significant other people. In effect, children learn to view themselves as distinct from the physical environment as well as from other people and do so by learning their relationships to various objects, spaces, and places including ownership, exclusion, limited access, and so on. Certain spaces and places, because they are "owned", familiar, and useful can be controlled, satisfy and maintain the integrity of the child's sense of self, including the definition of that self.'

Harold M. Proshansky and Abbé K. Fabian – 'Development of Place Identity in the Child', in Weinstein and David – *Spaces for Children*, 1987, p. 22.

RELATING TO THE WORLD

The world into which we are born, and within which as children we develop, is generally one that is more complex and multidimensional than a pristine beach. Our experience with otherwise untouched surroundings tends to be occasional and fleeting. During early development, as we become more mobile and aware, our first architectural challenges are to situate ourselves in relation to the built world of our rooms, houses and neighbourhoods. When young, those built surroundings constitute what we take to be our 'natural' environment.

Other factors come into play too. We interact (sometimes fight) with family and friends; and are sensibly circumspect about strangers. Time veers between darkness and light. There are warm places and cold. There is a difference between noise and music. Sometimes there are lovely or funny smells. We might be dimly aware of the always-remote horizon in the never-reachable distance but more conscious of a closer horizon (between matter and space) with which we are almost always (sometimes abruptly and painfully) in contact – the ground, which, whether dirt or carpet, is a constant datum and the prime arena of our place-making.

To understand our rudimentary relationships with the world we have to explore such subtleties in more detail.

FREE RANGE MOVEMENT
wandering as a cloud

On that pristine beach, a child running randomly is an image of unbridled freedom. Wide horizons, smooth sand, absence of obstacles – all in the context of clear air and bright sunshine – are conditions perfectly suited to an innocent spirit wanting to charge wildly in all directions, to relish its own burgeoning capacity for moving about.

These conditions are those provided by the desert too – the zone of nothingness, tracts of land with no organisation, without any spatial structure by which we might know where we are or where we are going. The open beach is an arena of freedom and fun, where kids can frolic like energetic ponies and gambol like frisky lambs. Its spatial liberality is in contrast with the structured organisation – the architecture – of the majority of the world in which we live.

On land that is featureless and open to the horizon in all directions, as children we might wander freely, run wildly, celebrate our physicality. But we could be lost in a desert.

Architecture gives structure to space. Through architecture we give structure to our surroundings, conjuring places sometimes from nowhere.

TARGETED MOVEMENT
going somewhere

Mostly our movements are neither wild nor free-ranging. Even as small children our movements are often targeted. With our hands we want that morsel of food or that toy. When we begin to crawl, it is so that we can reach a parent or pick up that fly dead on the floor.

As we gain confidence, the tracks we trace around the house and through its neighbourhood are conditioned, even dictated, by walls and doorways... We are partners in a dance, a (largely) silent interplay between our curiosity and desires, our capacity for movement, and the structured spaces we inhabit.

Ours is the melodic line; architecture provides the stave. Buildings set down routes, offer goals, provide rewards... Our lives are intertwined with and conditioned by architecture.

A child strides purposefully towards an intriguing doorway from which strange snorting noises are emanating. When I get there, will I be able to see what is on the other side? (Piglets actually.)

Though an open beach is fun (for a while), an architected environment can be more stimulating. It offers a framework within which to draw out narratives.

FOLLOWING PATHWAYS
going where I am led

Our world is a complex matrix of pathways. As children, we often move along paths laid down for us by others. We recognise and learn the architecture of the world those pathways establish. We get to know where particular pathways lead, what places they link. We trust established pathways to keep us safe; they tell us where we are and where we are going.

Sometimes we want to leave a pathway but the architecture – its edges – nudges us back. Sometimes we manage to deviate from the set path: it is 'at our own risk'. Most often we follow where we are led.

The influence and the metaphor of 'the pathway' – in life, in politics, in religious morality, in education and career progression... as well as in just travelling from one place to another – is clear.

We take pathways for granted; they are ubiquitous. Pathways dictate the routes we can take between places. They restrict our ability to wander freely. Pathways constitute a benevolent rule system. As children we learn to follow those rules. An architect determining the line of a pathway is like a parent holding a child's hand, or an authority laying down a law.

THRESHOLD CROSSING 1
stepping over

We get to learn that sometimes places are sharply separated by a dividing line, a threshold.

Thresholds separate distinct situations. When we cross a line we find ourselves in a different place. Some thresholds are inviting; some tricky. But sometimes crossing a threshold is forbidden. Like pathways, thresholds are parts in the language of architecture: punctuation.

When we are little, learning to walk confidently, we sometimes have to take great care. We learn to step over a raised threshold or climb stairs. With practice such tasks are sublimated. There are more interesting things to do and think about than stepping over a threshold or climbing stairs. Sometimes we miss the consequences.

As with the pathway, the metaphorical potential of the threshold is clear.

Sometimes we have to take care in the ways we negotiate our built environment. Crossing a simple threshold changes from being a challenge to being of no consequence as our confidence on our feet grows. Nevertheless, thresholds can be powerful in the transitions they present and the emotions they can elicit.

In 49 BCE, Julius Caesar crossed the Rubicon. In doing so he provoked civil war.

THRESHOLD CROSSING 2
out into the bright world

In gentle natural landscape thresholds may be subtle: maybe between water and dry land or sunlight and shade. In the environment we build for ourselves thresholds are (we seem keen to make them) more precise, more dramatic.

Our experience of the built world is punctuated by thresholds, lines between places, often between an inside and an outside. Such lines mark changes in circumstances. They elicit emotions: trepidation; excitement; relief...

To step over the threshold of a front door or a garden gate – from the ordered protective known realm of a house to the public exposed exterior – may be stimulating or it can be daunting.

As children we might not consciously acknowledge the power of a threshold but we are affected nevertheless.

To step across a threshold from inside to outside can be exciting or daunting. It can be like a young bird leaving its nest and learning to fly.

THRESHOLD CROSSING 3
into refuge, or dark mystery

Stepping over a threshold in the other direction
– from outside to inside – can elicit emotional
responses too.

    Returning home you shout 'Hi Mum' as you
pass through the doorway, and relax in the security
of your refuge.

    But if it is a strange doorway, through
which there is darkness and the unknown, then
crossing the threshold presents a challenge to be
overcome.

    A threshold is a powerful instrument in the
rudimentary architecture we make as children.
It is so in more sophisticated and permanent
architecture too.

*To step across a threshold
from outside to inside
might be a relief... or it
could be scary. We might
be returning to a known
refuge or venturing into an
unknown zone of threat.*

**As children and adults, our relationship with our surroundings is
emotional. Crossing thresholds elicits emotional responses.**

RECOGNISING
what's this, a place?

Wandering across a field without features, you encounter a square flat stone set in the grass. You recognise it as somehow special, different, distinct... a place.

It stimulates your curiosity. You question: what is it, why is it there, what might it be for? Maybe you wonder if it could be a place to stand. What would it be like standing on this flat stone?

You step onto the flat stone. You occupy it (opposite page). Now you are in a place that is distinct from the general everywhere. You feel different; somehow rooted. Even when you step off it, the stone feels like it is your place.

The stone is a tiny work of architecture: a place identified; a place open for occupation; a frame that you might adopt; a frame for you. A stage where you might sing or dance.

Our curiosity about the world means we are constantly interpreting things we see. Some of them are places we recognise as distinct from everywhere else, and which perhaps will lend themselves to particular purposes.

OCCUPYING
I put myself there

Our relationship with our environment is direct but seemingly subliminal. Quite young, without really thinking about it, we can find ourselves standing on a solitary paving stone – an island in a sea of grass – just because it is there.

Our interpretation of our surroundings becomes sublimated from our consciousness in a way similar to that in which we gradually develop such skill in language that we no longer have to think about each word or the structure of every sentence. Our intellectual relationship with our surroundings, in terms of interpretation at least, has becomes more or less automatic. We snap into conscious consideration of the places we occupy only when things get tricky…

To be an architect we need to be conscious about the power of place.

We are drawn to occupy places, to try them out, to root ourselves in them.

We had a cat who would precisely occupy loops of wire on the floor. Why? I don't know!

POSSESSING 1 – RECOGNISING
this is my place, the frame I choose and occupy

As children, we see something and want it. This desire can apply to a place as much as a thing (a toy or a piece of cake). You might want to sit in a particular seat at a table or climb on a rock and shout, 'I'm the king of the castle!'.

Possession is not necessarily assertive or aggressive. It may be no more than the temporary occupation of a place. In the above image a girl has recognised the archway in a hedge as a place. She has stopped there, and taken possession of it for the moment of posing for a photograph.

The photographer too has recognised the opening as a good frame for the child's picture. Her occupation of it is recorded for others to see.

As we move around we are constantly interpreting our surroundings, recognising and classifying places, and deciding what, if anything, to do with them. Sometimes we possess (occupy) the places we recognise only for the moment it takes for a camera's shutter to click. But that possession is recorded for posterity.

Architecture is about occupying frames. We choose and take possession of the frames we wish to inhabit.

POSSESSING 2 – CONFLICT
I shall fight for it

Possession of a place may be subject to dispute and conflict. Sometimes you feel that you have to defend or fight for the place you want to identify as your own.

Two brothers might tussle over who will sit in a particular chair. In other circumstances, battles over places (territories) can be more serious. Neighbours argue over boundaries and engage in feuds that can last for years. Nations go to war over disputed territory.

Identification of place by possession (i.e. architecture at its most fundamental) is a political, and sometimes aggressive, act.

As children we may fight over a chair. As adults things can escalate; we fight over territory.

Architecture can be about taking as well as making frames. Sometimes those frames become subjects of dispute.

MODIFYING, MAKING, INHABITING
I alter a place to make it better

A boy occupies a place suggested by a large piece of driftwood. He modifies it by collecting more driftwood and making a small fire. His place becomes a modest beach camp, framing him reading a book. He has also cooked and eaten some baked beans.

There are places for: fuel for the fire; the discarded tin; the tin opener; his cutlery... as well as for himself and the fire. These all relate to each other in subtle ways that include the zone of radiant warmth from the fire and the zone encompassed by the boy's reach.

All in all, by the minor modifications associated with his inhabitation, the boy has created a rudimentary dwelling place in which he can spend some time on the beach. It is the beginning of a house.

A boy makes a place for himself on the beach by modifying one suggested by a piece of driftwood that he recognises as a potential seat. He adjusts the driftwood to make it comfortable. He draws fuel for his fire nearby. His tools for eating – tin opener and cutlery – are at hand. He imbues the place with his inhabitation of it.

POINTING 1
I am here, but I relate myself to there

We are directional creatures. Our eyes point forwards. We align ourselves with things. The boy opposite is focussed on his book. When we move we propel ourselves in the direction upon which our eyes are fixed. When we make a place we orient it towards something – maybe the sun in the sky, a distant mountain or the horizon over the sea.

We are always pointing ourselves at things: towards our friends in conversation; idly staring at the telly... We set orientation in the places we make too.

POINTING 2
two projects by architecture students

When asked to make places in the landscape (almost as children) students can become selfconscious. Even so, their projects often involve pointing. The sense of establishing a link between a 'here' and the remote is engaging. Here is one example:

'Walking along the paths through the woodland, we came across an opening in the perimeter tree line. At this point we stopped and stood before a large stone between two tree trunks. The two trees acted as a frame within which we could view the picturesque landscape beyond. We sat on the stone, looking past the boulder covered field in the foreground to the wooded area beyond, and then to the hills and mountains in the far distance. From this point we were transported from the sheltered enclosure of the woodlands, through a window into the depths of the landscape.'

Ed O'Neill, Emily Dawson, James Cooper – 'The Projection of Layers', in Emily Dawson and William Quaile, eds. – *Landscape 2016*, Welsh School of Architecture, Cardiff, 2016.

This sense of linkage is powerful enough but the students wanted to intensify it. They decided to build a contraption to draw attention to the framed view…

The students' tutor was Zoë Berman. (See also page 78.)

'We wanted to extend the natural framework of the trees, and amplify the sense of being catapulted from the woodlands into the open expanse of the landscape.'

ibid.

… So the students built their own frame, which looked a bit like a drawn catapult (right, in plan).

Maybe, by not allowing you to stand in the significant spot yourself, the framework detracted from that sense of direct linkage with the remote you feel when standing before an opening. It dis-placed you. But the intention of this intervention was clear and powerful: the installation of architecture in the landscape to draw attention to and reinforce linkage between a 'here' and a 'there' by pointing. Similar syntactic devices have been used since ancient times: in burial mounds, temples, mosques, churches…

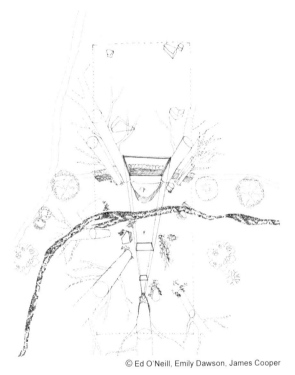

© Ed O'Neill, Emily Dawson, James Cooper

A second example was situated by the sea. A different group of students decided they had recognised a significant place where a sandy pathway crested a dune. Here, between swathes of marram grass, they built a doorway (right). The doorway established a link between that place and the infinitely remote horizon over the sea. It framed an encounter with that prospect. Climbing from the other direction, it also framed the moment when you became aware of the perfume of the pine forests behind the dune.

CHILDREN AS PLACE-MAKERS

37

MARKING
commemorating, associating

As children we mark the places of things that would otherwise be hidden from us. The hidden thing might be treasure or it might be the presence of something loved and lost – a dead pet... We might put the marker in a place associated with that lost pet – under its favourite tree for example – as a memorial.

As adults, we erect markers to represent abstract concepts such as national identity or the idea of loss. We put them in places associated with those concepts.

We might mark the grave of a dead pet with a stone in the shade of a protective tree.

'If we were to come across a mound in the woods, six foot long by three foot wide, with the soil piled up in a pyramid, a sombre mood would come over us and a voice inside us would say, "There is someone buried here". That is architecture.'

Adolf Loos, trans. Mitchell – 'Architecture' (1910), in Opel and Opel eds. – *On Architecture: Writings by Adolf Loos*, 2002.

PLACING
displaying, exhibiting, cherishing...

Assemblage, Merve Kaptan, 2018

We enjoy placing objects that interest us, or which we feel might be valuable (in whatever sense), on display, on 'altars'. This architectural act involves recognising or establishing a place suited to the purpose of display, and then the aesthetic act of choosing what to display and exactly how to arrange it.

Placing might be no more than the practical act of putting something on a shelf – or dresser or in a niche in a wall (right). But it might also involve imbuing the thing placed with reverence or love. Grandparents place photographs of their grandchildren in prominent locations on mantelpieces or sideboards... Religions place objects of veneration on altars...

Part of the sanctity of a family meal is due to its placement on a table...

We display things on mantelpieces and tables.

The provision of places to put things contributes to the sophistication of the prehistoric houses found at Skara Brae on Orkney.

HIDING
pretending I'm not here

Close your eyes and withdraw yourself inside your head. To do so is to escape from the world. The overload of sensory input from the eyes is shut off. With your eyes closed you are inside the room – the cell – of your own head. You can see things you would not normally notice.

As children we love to experiment with hiding. We do it for the fun of disappearing and re-emerging. We do it as if we are practising a survival skill. We also do it, as the drawings here suggest, with varying levels of success.

Sometimes it seems enough just to close our eyes. Maybe we think that if we cannot see the world, the world cannot see us. Certainly we can feel that we have gone into a different place just by closing our eyes. With them shut, it is as if our eyelids are a wall between us and the world. In this sense, just closing our eyes is an architectural act. It takes us to another place.

We play peekaboo, hiding behind our hands in front of our faces. Now those walls are our hands as well as our eyelids... walls which we demolish with a laugh!

Sometimes we find objects to hide behind. Maybe a book, or just a boot...

Or perhaps we 'hide' behind some coats hanging from their hooks, oblivious to the fact that our legs are showing.

Hiding is a favourite game for all children. Sometimes we do not realise that we are supposed to hide more than just our eyes and head.

**'All I want is a room somewhere
Far away from the cold night air...'** Alan Jay Lerner, from *My Fair Lady*, 1956.

We look for things in the world around us that we might be able to hide behind or inside. We hide behind doors or under sheets, behind trees or hedges...

Curtains are a favourite hiding place. We may be unaware that our toes are peeping out or of the bumps we make in the fabric. We like to hide but we also like to re-emerge, making our re-entrance as dramatic as possible.

At the supermarket we find crevices to squeeze into, causing concern in our parents.

At home we might see a 'cave' and try, unsuccessfully, to hide in it.

It seems that one of the traits deeply seated in our psychology is the awareness of the possibility of hiding. The desire to build hiding places – or at least places into which we can withdraw from the world – is one of the principal driving forces of architecture. After all, what is a house other than a place in which we can, for our own psychological health, hide ourselves from public view.

Maybe agoraphobia is not the principal motivation for architecture but it is certainly a factor. We want to hide from inclement weather; we want to protect ourselves from danger; we want to keep our things safe; we want privacy; sometimes we want to be alone with our own thoughts. Hiding is a life skill for which architecture provides a frame.

Sometimes we try to squeeze into places that are not quite big enough, or which we do not realise are betraying our concealed presence.

CHILD HIDING
Walter Benjamin

In the quotation below, the German Jewish philosopher Walter Benjamin describes the visceral relationship we, particularly as innocent children, can have with domestic places of concealment: places in which we hide; places where we dread discovery; places where we might find treasure; places we invest with magic, where we sense other – angelic or demonic – presences:

'He already knows all the hiding places in the apartment and returns to them as to a house where everything is sure to be just as it was. His heart pounds, he holds his breath. Here he is enclosed in the world of matter. It becomes immensely distinct, speechlessly obtrusive. In such manner does a man who is being hanged become aware of the reality of rope and wood. Standing behind the doorway curtain, the child becomes something floating and white, a ghost. The dining table under which he is crouching turns him into a wooden idol in a temple whose four pillars are the carved legs. And behind a door he is himself a door, wears it as his heavy mask and as a shaman will bewitch all those who unsuspectingly enter. At no cost must he be found. When he pulls faces, he is told, the clock need only strike and he will remain so. The element of truth in this he finds out in his hiding place. Anyone who discovers him can petrify him as an idol under the table, weave him forever as a ghost into the curtain, banish him for life into the heavy door. And so, at the seeker's touch he drives out with a loud cry the demon who has so transformed him – indeed, without waiting for the moment of discovery, he grabs the hunter with a shout of self-deliverance. That is why he does not tire of the struggle with the demon. In this struggle the apartment is the arsenal of his masks. Yet once each year, in mysterious places, in their empty eye-sockets, their fixed mouths, presents lie. Magic discovery becomes science. As its engineer the child disenchants the gloomy parental apartment and looks for Easter eggs.'

Walter Benjamin, trans. Jephcott and Shorter – 'One-Way Street' (1925–6), in *One-Way Street and Other Writings*, 1985.

During the Second World War, a German Jewish girl called Anne Frank spent just over two years hiding from the Gestapo in concealed rooms in a building in Amsterdam. She and her family were discovered in August 1944 and sent to concentration camps where Anne and her sister Margot died. Anne recorded the period of her family's hiding in *The Diary of a Young Girl* (1947).

A PRIVATE DARK WORLD
for watching YouTube

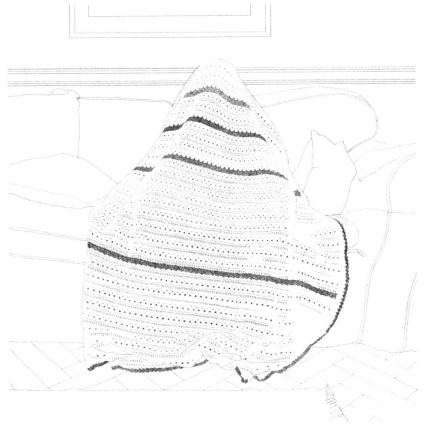

Sometimes, as children, we hide for a purpose; to escape from the world around. It is a cliché to 'hide behind the sofa' when something frightening comes on television. We might hide when we just want to be with ourselves, to relax, to concentrate on some problem… Here (above) my granddaughter has withdrawn from company to focus on watching a YouTube video on her iPad. In doing so she has made her own cinema, a dark enclosed refuge with a screen upon which a different world is being shown. So far as she is concerned, she is no longer in the company of the rest of the family. She is on her own.

A child makes a place by hiding away from the world… maybe just to be on her own, or perhaps to have darkness to concentrate on a video.

Plato, in his 'metaphor of the cave' (see the *Metaphor* Notebook pages 118–19), suggested the unenlightened are chained in caves and see only shadows projected on its walls (or tablet screens?).

PEEPING AND PEERING
seeing without being seen

Peeping is associated with hiding – a consequent pleasure; you have to hide (if only behind your hands) before you can peep. And peeping is a way of hiding whilst also being in contact with the world from which you are concealed. The combination amuses both the hider and those from whom he or she is hidden.

Peeping may be an architectural verb itself. We build peeping into the hiding places of our houses. Windows may let sunlight and air into a dark interior but they are also the openings through which we peep from within our refuge to see visitors arriving or to spy nosily on our neighbours.

Large fortresses – ultimate refuges – are built with small peep-holes (loop-holes) through which to spot advancing enemies and fire arrows or muskets at them.

Peeping – either from within or from without – is a way of pricking the bubble of isolation inflated by hiding or exclusion. Paranoia prompts peeping – spying – between nations' secret services.

BEING IN ANOTHER PLACE
playing with separation

As children we are fascinated by being in places separated from our family.

    A child might run through a gate to peer and wave at her grandfather through the railings – to experience and enjoy being in a different place from him. The fence is not a threshold but a barrier, a wall through which neither he nor she may pass. The instrument of separation is the fence – an architectural element.

    There is a thrill in the separation that can only be interpreted as an experiment in what child psychologists call individuation, a process which will develop into her being happy to be herself, to be alone in a place by herself without the supervision of parents or carers... a place to be mischievous?! Architecture provides the spatial matrix for such experiments.

A child waves at its grandfather through the railings she has just run behind. She enjoys the sensation of being in 'another place' but one with the security of also being able to see the presence of a protective adult. She is playing with separation. The instrument of separation is an architectural element – the fence.

SIGNING
establishing a persisting link with a place

Across the world prehistoric cave art displays examples of us wanting to record our presence in particular places – maybe by leaving stencilled silhouettes of our hands – and thereby establish personal lasting relationships with them.

The visitors book of a cave in France shows children doing exactly the same – drawing outlines of their hands to record their visit. Church visitors might do something similar by lighting a candle. In other places we might clap our hands, bang a gong, meditate… all to establish links between ourselves and the spirits of those places.

SIGNING
setting a link with place in concrete, literally

A palm print, stencil, outline or impression in concrete is one of the most personal ways in which we can sign a place. By doing this we know that our presence in the place will persist for a long time, maybe even beyond our own death.

Such a signature is a modest way of marking a place. But the same impulse can be behind much more elaborate and expensive ventures, such as when a political dictator deems that their nation's new airport should be named after him. Such a diktat identifies the dictator's identity with that of the country at its most significant location, its portal of entry and exit.

Less ominously, children – young and old – seem drawn to leaving impressions of their hands pressed into wet concrete. Such are seals of a sort of ownership.

A palm illicitly pressed into unset concrete produces a signature that will persist for many years. (This example is in Dundee.)

A palm print on a dirty bus window is more ephemeral.

DIGGING HOLES
down into the sand

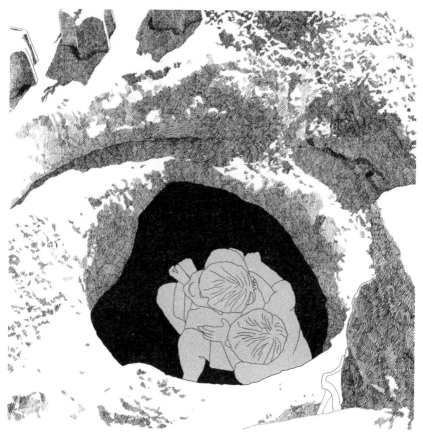

Sand is easy to dig. Damp, it stays in shape. This makes it good for making sandcastles. It also means that holes can be dug. Apart from provoking well-meaning passers-by to tease, 'You'll come out in Australia!' (or wherever lies on the opposite side of the globe), holes offer a new kind of place, one in which you can hide, one in which you get a new perspective on the world.

Holes, poetically, are tombs and places where we can escape danger. Nuclear bunkers are, essentially, holes in the ground where the threats of blast and radiation cannot reach.

Oblivious to the mortal danger of being buried alive, these boys (above) are giggling at the sensation of being in the hole they have dug for themselves.

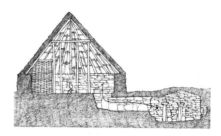

In prehistoric Orkney, people dug 'earth houses' attached to their homes. It is thought these were used for cold storage and for hiding during times of threat.

RELATIONSHIPS WITH THE HORIZON
Sverre Fehn

'My interest has always been where to put man in relation to the horizon in a built environment... Everything we build must be adjusted in relation to the ground, thus the horizon becomes an important aspect of architecture... Where between heaven and earth do I place people?'

Sverre Fehn, in Per Olaf Fjeld
– Sverre Fehn: the Pattern of Thoughts, 2009.

If Black Holes have 'event horizons' (as cosmologists suggest) then our land has a horizon not only in the unreachable distance but also between its matter and the space above it in which we live. We call that horizon the ground's surface. As Sverre Fehn suggests, architecture is an instrument for manipulating our relationship with both types of horizon.

This sense of architecture as an instrument for managing relationships with horizons is evident in the places we make as children.

It is by the language of architecture that we position ourselves in relation to the surface of the earth. The boys opposite have positioned themselves below it, in their hole; their relationship with the remote horizon is closed off by their situation below the horizon of matter and space.

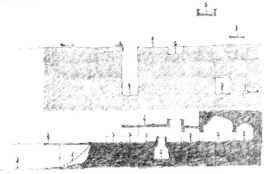

We can have different relationships with the remote horizon. We might find ourselves in open land with a clear view of that unreachable horizon all around. We might be within a cave with a view of the horizon only through its open mouth.

We can have different relationships with the horizon that is the surface of the earth. We might find ourselves standing upon it – the normative state. We might be in a hole up to our waist, in which situation we have a different relationship. We might be up to our eyes, with a tangential view across the earth's surface. We might stand on a surface that is raised – some sort of platform that lifts us above the ordinary everyday level of the ground – or high on a rock or tower, in which case our relationship with the ground is broken or at least stretched. When as children we dig or climb, we are playing with our relationship with horizons.

We can position ourselves in relation to the horizon by digging holes or standing on rocks.

All architecture – its floors, cellars, roofs, verandas... – plays with our relationship with the remote horizon and the horizon between earth and space.

REFUGE...
withdrawing from the world...

The geographer Jay Appleton* has argued that our appreciation of the landscape is conditioned by our experience of refuges with prospect – combining protection and view. This combination of refuge and prospect is important in architecture, even the rudimentary sort we make as children.

A child hides behind a chair, appreciating the refuge it provides; but he also wants to be able to see what is happening elsewhere.

'There was nowhere as safe as Fortress Caparetto in the whole of Garmouth. Above the thin steel of the Anderson's arched roof were three solid feet of earth and rockery, concreted together here and there. It would have withstood anything but a direct hit from the Bismarck. An old patchwork quilt kept draughts from the door... Chas's heart glowed with pride... They worked on the garden, too, directing the waters of the tiny stream with dams, so that the whole area became an ankle-deep swamp through which no one could pass.'

* Jay Appleton – *The Experience of Landscape*, 1975.

Robert Westall – *The Machine Gunners*, 1975.

... AND PROSPECT
... but being able to see threats and opportunities

In his book *The Machine Gunners*, Robert Westall describes a gun emplacement constructed by some boys to repel enemy airplanes in the war. It had to combine refuge – being hidden – with prospect – being able to see the planes to shoot.

'Beyond, lay the machine-gun emplacement, walled with pongy sandbags and floored with a framework of boards... The gun-emplacement was roofed in with old doors and soil. Only the three loop-holes for the gun showed from the outside, and that was the way you got in. At the other side, they fixed a whole section of fence so it would fall outward when someone pulled a rope from inside the Fortress. That gave what Lieutenant Andrew Morgan had called a good field of fire. Audrey uprooted plants and privet-bushes and planted them on top for camouflage.'

A boy eats an apple, sitting in the refuge he has made for himself with driftwood, enjoying the prospect of the ocean and lands across the water on the distant horizon.

Robert Westall – *The Machine Gunners*, 1975.

EARTH AND AIR
matter's reciprocation with space

'The elements of the house can be derived only from nature; the primary datum of the wall-separated space is the unlimited mass of the earth with the limitless space above it; so the limited mass of the walls must also be drawn from the earth in order to withdraw a limited piece of space from the space of nature.'

Dom H. van der Laan, trans. Padovan – *Architectonic Space*, 1983.

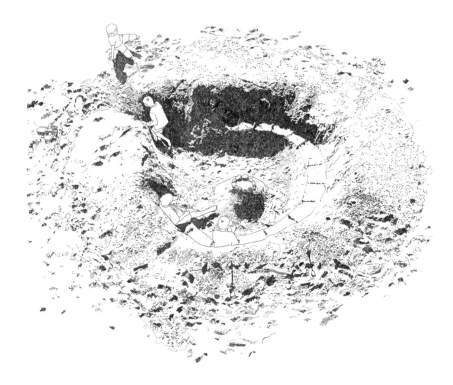

Here is an example of the point van der Laan makes in the quotation above. The positive occupiable place in the drawing is made by taking material from the ground's surface – sand mounded into the place's earthwork walls. 'The limited mass of the walls (is) drawn from the earth to withdraw a limited piece of space from the space of nature'. This reciprocal relationship between matter and space is particularly evident in beach places but it applies to other, more sophisticated, architecture too.

The social circle this place also establishes is discussed on page 140.

'The child holds himself up with the help of its mother's leg, the first column in its life. The child conquers and conquers, walls, doors, the toilet, everything. It grows into the room and becomes the little individual that forms the world.'

Sverre Fehn quoted in Per Olaf Fjeld - *Sverre Fehn: The Pattern of Thoughts*, 2009, p. 104.

PLACE CREATION

We are constantly weighing up the world around us. Most of the time we do this without consciously thinking about it. In the countryside, we consider where to walk, where to place our feet. We look out for places that might trip us up or suck us into a bog. We look for somewhere dry and clean to sit, somewhere reasonably comfortable to lie down, a shady spot out of the hot sun. Playing games we might search for somewhere to hide from friends, or a tree trunk to use as cricket stumps. In the city we recognise that it is safer to walk on the pavement than in the middle of the road. We recognise somewhere to buy sweets or have a coffee, somewhere just to sit in the sun and watch people walking by, or to shelter from the rain. All these instances are aspects of our innate faculty for place recognition. But recognition also confers identification. We conjure up places from our surroundings. And by doing so we give our world architecture.

NATURAL SETTING AS BUILDING
living on a rocky outcrop

These families have converted the rocky margins of a beach into an inhabitation for their day by the sea. They have found places to sit, to climb, to play. They have turned space behind a boulder into a changing room. The top of another rock is a dining room for three boys eating their sandwiches. Three girls sit on steps in the rock eating theirs. Towels and wetsuits are laid out to dry in the sun, toys strewn randomly on the ground. Cups sit on natural shelves. For the duration of their day on the beach this inhabitation becomes home.

As children we can see the natural environment as building, ready for inhabitation. We can recognise places in a natural rocky outcrop as places suited for different purposes: sitting, climbing, changing, drying towels…

As children, our relationship with our surroundings is creative. Our innate capacity for architecture interprets the world in terms of places.

BUILDING AS NATURAL SETTING
interpreting a wall as a rocky outcrop

To these children, the face of a building is as much a piece of nature as a beach cliff. The verbs of architecture, as they pertain to our experience of the world as children, straddle both the natural and the human-made environment.

The drawing above is based on a photograph by Neil Libbet taken in 1971. It illustrates an attribute we human beings share with just about all living creatures – animals and plants – our capacity for finding place for ourselves involving recognition and occupation. This capacity is the origin of all architecture. These children could be birds, monkeys, goats, weeds or tree saplings… insinuating themselves onto the precarious hand-, root- and footholds of this building's façade (The Black-E Arts Centre in Liverpool).

The capacity for identifying place – place-making – involves our intuitive cognition, our ability to recognise place opportunities – a wall to sit on or a ledge on which to stand precariously – all without involving any verbal or mathematical reasoning or calculation.

As children we can see the built environment as a natural landscape. Low walls become seats or pathways. Walls with ledges and window sills become cliffs for climbing. Their surfaces become rock faces for the timeless primitive art of graffiti.

We make natural surroundings artificial and interpret artificial surroundings as if they were natural.

We recognise a cave as a place to shelter from sun or rain, as a place to explore, as a place to conceal treasure or to hide one's self. Enticing and scary at the same time, as a place that is mysterious a cave provokes the imagination into inventing stories of prehistoric times, of pirates and smugglers, of monsters waiting to gobble you up. A cave becomes architecture when you see it as a place: for yourself, for a monster, for the conjuring of a story... Without you and your imagination it is no more than a fissure in the rock. (At least that is what it is to a geologist rather than a child.)

ROCK SHELTERS 1
sitting in the shade

Our prehistoric selves lived in rock shelters (left) rather than caves. These provided refuge from sun and rain whilst enjoying light and an open prospect of the surrounding land with its threats and opportunities.

    Our modern selves find 'rock shelters' to inhabit too. When it rains we run into a nearby doorway or under the ineffective leaves of a tree. The sheltered porch outside the plant room of our local library (below) has been a favourite 'cave' for young people to sit, chat, smoke…

In prehistoric times we lived sheltering under overhanging cliffs.

Nowadays we find ad hoc shelters, when we need them, in our towns and cities.

ROCK SHELTERS 2
sheltering from the storm

'There is shadow under this red rock. (Come in under the shadow of this red rock.)'

T.S. Eliot – 'The Waste Land' (1922).

Finding places in our surroundings is our basic architectural impulse. In the shade of a rocky overhang at the base of Uluru (Ayer's Rock; right) children were taught about their world with the wall as blackboard.

In the contemporary world, those without the resources to find themselves a fixed abode have to find places to rest. They choose the urban equivalent of rock shelters – the doorways, porches, recesses… of modern buildings (below).

People without orthodox homes make them for themselves with cardboard and blankets in shop doorways.

ANALYSING ARCHITECTURE NOTEBOOKS

Children sitting under a tree have committed an act of architecture. They have recognised and adopted it as a place, a place that is identified by the trunk at its centre, the overhanging canopy of the branches and leaves and the circle of shadow cast on the ground. These are the elements of the place's architecture, as created by the children's recognition and imagination aided by the tree itself. Without the children, or their recognition of it as such, the tree would not constitute architecture. (It would just be, to a botanist, whatever species of tree it is.)

UNDER A TREE
shade in the midday sun

The basic elements of a house and temple are present in a tree. The trunk and branches are its structure; the canopy of leaves its roof; the shadow on the ground is its floor and the edge of that shadow its threshold.

    Crossing the shadow threshold you enter a place, a special place. You recognise it as such, as you anticipated it would be when you saw the tree from a distance. Entering under it 'restores your soul'. The tree, as a house, is a refuge like your mother's arms.

    You can relax under the tree, surveying the world from your refuge of shade.

    Such places have mysterious powers. They are where fairies and spirits live. They are where stories are told. The places under trees are where dreams are to be had.

A spreading tree is a house and temple…

UNDER A TREE
a place to sleep, perchance to dream

'*A spring evening, so brightly moonlit that one could have seen to read, and the leaves of the single tree there standing, an ancient and mighty terebinth, short trunked, with strong and spreading branches, stood out fine and sharp against the light... This beautiful tree was sacred. In more than one way enlightenment was to be had within its shadow: from the mouth of man, for whoever through personal experience had aught to communicate of the divine would gather hearers together under its branches; but likewise in more inspired manner. For persons who slept leaning their heads against the trunk had repeatedly been vouchsafed dispensations and commands in a dream; and at the offering of burnt sacrifices... the behaviour of the smoke, the flight of birds, or even a sign from heaven itself had often, in the course of the years, proved that a peculiar efficacy lay in these pious doings at the foot of the tree.*'

... a refuge, a place to dream, for spells and sacrifices.

Thomas Mann, trans. Lowe-Porter – *The Tales of Jacob*, in *Joseph and His Brothers* (1933), 1999.

UNDER A TABLE
a ready-made domain

A favourite child place is the space under a table. We have probably all done it, hiding or inhabiting the space like a room or house. It is worth reflecting on what makes going under a table interesting or attractive. It seems to be that feeling of being sheltered, protected, enclosed, framed... that lies at the very core of our innate architectural capacity. All architecture is about frame-making. Temples frame gods or altars. Aedicules frame kings or tombs. Four-poster beds frame wedding couples. Our rooms frame our lives. A table is a ready-made frame waiting for our occupation.

'The White table is big... in the lower story, I lived from the moment I learned to crawl on all fours. It was like a large market place where I ruled all by myself.'

The artist Rachel Whiteread has drawn attention to the space beneath furniture by making it solid (below).

Alvar Aalto, quoted in Schildt – *Alvar Aalto: The Early Years*, 1997.

ANALYSING ARCHITECTURE NOTEBOOKS

IN A CAGE
a strange, but secure, place to be

When my daughter's family acquired a small dog they also bought a cage in which it could sleep. The attraction of a frame as a place in which to situate oneself is illustrated by my grandson's happy desire to crawl into the dog's cage. Imagine the intensity of that quintessential architectural experience. One might feel it entering a small shed in open countryside and closing the door. Imagine the emotional effect of such containment. Containment cures agoraphobia... or provokes claustrophobia.

'Will Hamilton liked his glass cage of an office in the garage... He loved the movement that went on outside his square glass cage... He sat in his big red leather swivel chair, and most of the time he enjoyed his life.'

My grandson has crawled inside the family dog's cage. He is enjoying (honestly, he is) the experience of being framed in this see-through container; maybe also of identifying with the dog – putting himself in its place (literally). But he knows he can get out. The door is not bolted, and his mother is there (capturing him with the photograph).

John Steinbeck – *East of Eden* (1952), 2000.

HOUSE
turning the world upside down

Occupying the space under a table can be a communal activity. The space under a table is a distinct place where a small group of friends can define their cohesion spatially, architecturally, and by telling stories. The space under a table is a safe place separated from adults.

'Whenever the younger children in the school had an opportunity, they would arrange the chairs and tables so as to make a "cosy place" with a defensive rampart... the defensive element comes out clearly here and there – "so that nobody can look in", or "to keep the foxes out". Sometimes the children added to the intensity of their feeling of security by asking a grown-up to "be a tiger – and come from a distance, so that we can hear you growling".'

A table, or at least the space under it, offers the possibility of occupation as a house.

Susan Isaacs – *Social Development in Young Children* (1933), 1999.

SCHOOL
on the stairs

My granddaughter likes to play school on the stairs. I do not really know why she always chooses the stairs. She is usually the teacher. Maybe the elevation provided by the stairs gives her a sense of superiority. She is also quite authoritarian, often imposing the 'naughty step' as a punishment.

'Halfway down the stairs
is a stair where I sit.
There isn't any
other stair quite like it.'
A.A. Milne – *When We Were*
Very Young, 1924.

PRESENCE AND PERFORMANCE
imagining a stage

We recognise the places conjured up by the presence of other people. We recognise the space they occupy with their life – movement, presence, aura, performance, vitality. We acknowledge and relate to the bubble they generate around themselves.

When a clown performs in a field the space around him is transformed into a stage by his presence and his performance.

Intuitively we recognise the stage implied by the clown's performance. We define its boundaries by forming an audience around its periphery. Together we create a complete theatre, minus the building.

'All the world's a stage,
And all the men and women merely players.'

We relate ourselves to the auras, the bubbles of presence others generate around themselves. We do this with performers; we do it with each other too.

The world we inhabit is covered with many layers of circles of place; some fixed; many more – centred on us as individuals – mobile. Sometimes architecture concretes those circles of place (see page 138).

William Shakespeare – *As You Like It* (1623), Act 2:7.

APPROPRIATING A STAGE
reinterpreting a defined area of ground

Alternatively a child might encounter a few old paving stones in front of a grown-over gateway in a hedge and reinterpret them as a stage, appropriating them for an impromptu performance.

Such behaviour seems to reinforce the idea that we possess an innate language of architecture. Not only does the child recognise the paving stones as a distinct place, which she identifies as a place for performance. She also, subliminally (to use an appropriate term), seems attuned to the associated 'ghost' gateway as a place of emergence, of entrance into the outer world, like the proscenium arch of a theatre.

Beneath such simple acts of natural abandon – the child dancing on the paving stones – lies a subtle and sophisticated capacity for architecture.

A child, by her dance, converts some old paving stones into a stage. Just by being, and by being alive, as children we change the world.

A STAGE FOR DARING
for showing off

Sometimes we, as children, look for stages for more dramatic – challenging and daring – performances.

On sunny days boys and girls (above) come down to the harbour to jump off the end into the sea. The lower the tide, the higher, and therefore more daring, the jump. The performance involves thrill but also showing-off. The harbour, the weather, the state of the tide... and the presence of an audience ... all contribute to the architecture of the stage.

Whatever age we are, we are constantly interpreting the world around us, on the lookout for places we might use, sometimes inventing purposes for places with particular characteristics.

By doing these things we are constantly reinventing the world with our own narratives.

A group of friends – competitors too – recognise the end of the harbour as a good place for a thrill, and to show off... to each other and to tourists standing around.

We like to interact with the world. We look for opportunities suggested by places. We recognise places and think what we might enjoy doing with them, in them, from them...

ROPE SWING
flying

Sometimes we, as children, make places that stretch our relationships with the ground and with gravity.

We recognise the possibilities of a rope hanging from the branch of a tree. A rope swing (almost) gives us the sensation of flying through the air, free of the restrictions of pedestrian horizontal movement across the ground held down by gravity. We can even let go of it at the end of its arc, to fly gracefully (?) into the waters of a lake or river.

As children we enjoy the drama of varying sensations; the thrill of risk; the sensory stimulation of air, movement, immersion...

(Perhaps more staid architecture does not exploit such desire for sensation and stimulation? Maybe it could?)

A rope swing allows you to explore the tenuous boundaries of your relationship with the ground.

KING OF THE CASTLE
this is my realm

Boys climb a rock because it is there.

   The rock presents a challenge and the possibility of achievement. Reaching the top is the objective. From below it is seen as a place where you will feel special. When you are there you see the world from a superior perspective – you are the 'king of the castle'. You are the embryo of a fortress that, on just one short day by the sea, you do not actually get to build.

   Scaling the rock involves recognising other places too. In climbing you have to find a pathway, a rudimentary staircase, by which to find a route to the top. When the tide is in, the rock provides ledges from which to leap into the sea too (as of the harbour on page 68).

   The rock stimulates an architectural dialogue between you and it.

We identify the summit of a distinctive rock as a place of aspiration. We enjoy the challenge of climbing to the top and the achievement of getting there to survey the world around.

PROJECTION OF POWER
I can see, and be seen from, everywhere

Buildings – churches, fortresses… – are placed at the top of pinnacles of rock as manifestations of the presence of a person or institution. They exploit the architecture of the rock. As pilgrims or attackers we must find a route to the summit; to reach closer to heaven or to the centre of power. The summit presents a challenge and the possibility of achievement. It is a target of aspiration.

    The rock also provides the individual or the institution with a locus of domination. By taking possession of the rock's summit, he, she or it becomes, literally or metaphorically, the lord (militarily, religiously, politically…) of all it surveys.

    The child's playful ascent to the top of a craggy rock is the father of a political statement expressed in architecture.

Powerful individuals or institutions use the architecture of a distinctive rock – its summit and challenging ascent – to exaggerate their presence and project their power across the land.

SPREADING ON THE ROCKS
settling in

Rocks at the base of a sea cliff may not seem to offer a comfortable setting in which to settle. But sometimes we can defy conditions.

Through our capacity for interpreting such rough complexity we might find a place to lie reasonably comfortably in the sun. We are attuned to finding anthropomorphic harmony between our own bodily form and the natural settings in which we find ourselves, whether just sitting leaning against a tree trunk or adjusting our bodies to uneven rocks.

Of course one's recognition of such a setting as an appropriate place to settle should also take into account the possibility of rocks falling from the cliffs above. But to insinuate yourself into such an unpromising setting is a subtle act of architecture.

Our capacity for architecture is capable of recognising and occupying (identifying) places to settle in unlikely settings… especially when we want to soak up some sun.

SETTLING ON THE ROCKS
accommodating to topography

We can do exactly the same thing with more permanent architecture. We do not always choose flat even sites for building.

The challenging and dramatic setting of the Casa Malaparte (c. 1937; Adalberto Libera/Curzio Malaparte) on the island of Corfu is essential to its power and charm as a work of architecture.

The Casa Malaparte (above) is a child's response to landscape, not because it is naive but because it illustrates an intuitive grasp of the powers (to refer to the verbs of architecture outlined in the first chapter) of recognition and placing supplemented by modification and building, all in the cause of occupation.

The house is a metaphor too: a fortress, a ship beneath a flat deck, a poet's retreat from the world*... all at once.

Our ability to build in unlikely locations derives from our innate capacity to recognise place even in seemingly difficult settings.

The Casa Malaparte was used as a location in the movie *Le Méspris* (Jean-Luc Godard, 1963; aka, in English, *Contempt*).

* See the *Metaphor Notebook*, pages 61–2.

PATHWAY 1
wandering or finding a route through a labyrinth

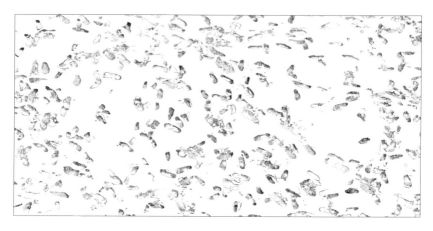

On an open beach we can wander where we wish.

In other circumstances we have to negotiate a pathway through obstacles.

A small boy wonders what route to take through so many strangers.

PATHWAY 2
being led, following authority

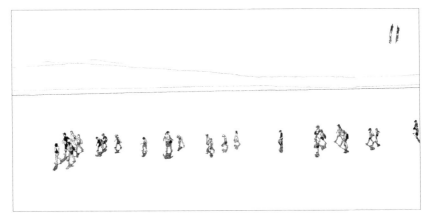

As children, we have various relationships with pathways. These can be interpreted metaphorically (in ways ranging from freedom, through benevolent channelling, to subservience) but initially they are just to do with our architectural relationships with the physical world.

On an open beach (opposite, top) we wander, and our pathways freely cross those of others. In a landscape of obstacles, whether natural or human-made (opposite, below) we must negotiate our own pathway through the labyrinth. Sometimes (above) we follow the pathway established by someone in authority. And gradually, as we grow, we learn to follow the pathways laid down and fixed for us by the established architecture of playground, garden or city (below).

Sometimes we follow a pathway determined by a leader.

Our footsteps identify the pathways we tread. They record our foot size and footwear, our rough age, our pace, our gait, our weight, and our direction, which is governed by our goal. They manifest our passing presence and suggest our purpose.

We learn to follow pathways laid down by architecture.

PATHWAY 3
following the way

Much of our world is organised for us by pathways. Pathways link places; they also determine the routes that may be taken between them.

As children we learn the power of laid-down pathways. We do so without really thinking about the authority they hold over us and our movements. Laid-down pathways establish the rules of our wanderings just as powerfully as (if not more so than) the laws of the land prescribe what we can or cannot do.

Pathways, whether on land or sea, or high in the air, create a complicated interlaced matrix of routes by which we find our way from one place to another, near or far. As children we learn them to understand the structure and accessibility of our surroundings.

A girl rides her trike along a pathway. Her route is determined for her. She chooses to follow it because she wishes to get to where it leads.

She also interprets the lane as possessing its own inherent character as a place: 'spooky!'. And imposes a password at the gate into the distant park.

'I know where I'm going. I know who's going with me.'
Traditional ballad.

PATHWAY 4
walking on walls

As children we enjoy being inventive, testing the boundaries of established (conventional) place definition.

A wall is quintessentially an architectural element the purpose of which is to create a barrier between one place and another. But, as children, we challenge that definition by re-conceptualising its top surface as a pathway.

Walking precariously along the top of a wall, maybe or maybe not holding the hand of a parent, is a stimulating experience physically. Our head height is nearer that of an adult. We worry about falling off. We enjoy the test of our own physical prowess. But subliminally we also enjoy the challenge to the orthodox architectural definition of a wall and its reinvention as its conceptual opposite – a pathway.

A child walks confidently along the top of a wall. The wall has been reinvented as a pathway. The conceptual twist involved entertains the child, along with the physical stimulation of precarious balance, and becoming the same height as an adult.

We can reinvent a pavement as a track for a race against our siblings, a stair as a descent into hell or a ladder to heaven… We can interpose stories between us and the world.

PLACES ALONG A ROUTE
narrative mapping

My granddaughter and I sometimes walk to the shops, about ten minutes from our house. We take various routes. Each has its own places – with names or particular activities associated with them – on the way. There is the place where we pass either side of parked cars peeping at each other through their windows. There is the house where the dog barks. There is the scary lane, sometimes avoided, sometimes relished. There are places – gateways – where passwords have to be invented. There is the place where we used to have to crouch down to wait for the green man to allow us to cross the road…

'With the first steps of the ancestors across the land, country was sung into creation.'
Alexis Wright – 'Talking about Country', in Sarina Singh and others – *Aboriginal Australia & the Torres Strait Islands*, 2001.

All of us – as children, route finders, mental cartographers… – make narrative maps of the surroundings we inhabit. We make sense of our world with them. Australian Aborigine culture 'sings songs' telling stories about particular places and their mythical relationships dating from the Dreamtime. These 'songlines' form narrative maps by which places are identified.

In 2016 some students at the Welsh School of Architecture set about making interventions in the landscape. One is shown on pages 36–7. Another group* was alive to the narrative dimension of walking through the countryside. Sensitive to places with particular character along a route, they set about intensifying them. Their main material was string. They produced a series of interventions, orchestrating a walker's experience of the landscape, in both broad and intimate ways. The last of the series provided the walker with a rest and opportunity for reflection:

'We inhabited an encased space created by a large boulder that had been split in half. The user was encouraged to sit within this void and face a large internal surface of rock. Hidden away and out of sight from the main path, the only evidence of this intervention was the string wrapped over the south-facing surface of the rock. On the other side this string created a canopy effect above a moss-covered rock acting as a seat. This moment provided a quiet space for reflection at the end of the journey.'

Uluru (Ayer's Rock) in central Australia is traditionally 'mapped' in terms of 'songs' linking particular places with events from the distant path (above).

See: Charles P. Mountford – *Ayers Rock*, 1965; also the *Metaphor* Notebook, pages 153–4.

* The students' tutor was again Zoë Berman.

Sion Riley, Roshni Patel, William Quaile – 'Moments on a Journey', in Emily Dawson and William Quaile, eds. – *Landscape 2016*, Welsh School of Architecture, Cardiff, 2016.

INTANGIBLE PLACE IDENTIFIERS 1
light... or is it dark?

'Where shall I set the candles?' 'Oh – oh, anywhere...' 'How about here on the floor? Any objections?' 'No.'

'I can't hardly see you sitting way over there.' 'I can see you.' 'I know, but that's not fair, I'm in the limelight.'
Tennessee Williams – *The Glass Menagerie* (1945), 2009.

Songlines, narrative maps, involve the intangible element of time. As children, our place-making, in its ephemerality, is generally timeless. Out in the world of day it equally generally tends not to involve itself in the manipulation of light. But in still darkness, outside or in a room, our rudimentary architecture can enlist that intangible element.

The simplest, most rudimentary architectural form composed of light is the sphere of illumination, imperceptibly fading to its periphery, of a candle in darkness. Safer is the sphere of light provided by a lantern or the cone of light directed by a torch under a bed sheet. More fickle is the light from a firework or sparkler.

'A candle just brought gradually lit up the study and its familiar details became visible.'
Leo Tolstoy, trans. Maude – *Anna Karenina* (1878), 1995.

A girl opposite me on the train was looking at her phone. The carriage, which had no internal lights, went into a dark tunnel. The girl's face was lit only by her phone's screen.

INTANGIBLE PLACE IDENTIFIERS 2
warmth... or is it cold?

A fire is one of the quintessential place identifiers. A fire has prehistoric originality, eternal valency, timeless poetry. As children we are fascinated by making a fire on the beach or in the woods. The collection of fuel and attempts at lighting result in satisfying conflagration, as if some primeval force had been unleashed.

Children gather around a fire on the beach as a place of warmth and a place to cook food. The hearth also becomes a centre of their shared world and a focus of their communality.

The principal purpose of a fire – besides those emotional effects suggested above – is to provide heat to fend off cold and cook food. At night a fire also provides light (see previous page) and aroma (see next page).

If you wanted to cite the most powerful example of a child-made place it would be a fire in the landscape.

'Howling round the pyre they helped each other all night long to fan the flames...'

Homer, trans. Rieu – *The Iliad* (c. 700 BCE), 1950.

ANALYSING ARCHITECTURE NOTEBOOKS

INTANGIBLE PLACE IDENTIFIERS 3
smell... or is it perfume?

Nappies stink (sometimes), baking bread makes our mouths water, bad places smell bad, the comforting embrace of a mother or father might smell of perfume... We identify places with smell as well as by sight and association. As children we light a fire in the woods as much for the aroma of the burning wood as for warmth or light.

Smells provoke memories. I remember my mother's roasting beef. Juhani Pallasmaa remembers his grandfather's farmhouse by its smell:

> 'I cannot remember the appearance of the door to my grandfather's farmhouse in my early childhood, but I do remember the resistance of its weight and the patina of its wood surface scarred by decades of use, and I recall especially vividly the scent of home that hit my face as an invisible wall behind the door. Every dwelling has its individual smell of home.'

Juhani Pallasmaa – *The Eyes of the Skin*, 2005.

By smells we can identify – recognise – places. The novelist Gabriel García Márquez remembered how his blind Aunt Petra found her way about the house:

> 'She lived in the room next to the office, where the workshop was later, and she developed a magical skill for moving around in her darkness without anyone's help. I still remember her as if it was yesterday, walking without a stick as if she had both eyes, slow but without hesitation, guided only by different smells. She recognized her room by the vapor of muriatic acid in the workshop next door, the hallway by the perfume of jasmines in the garden, my grandparents' bedroom by the smell of wood alcohol they both would rub on their bodies before they went to sleep, Aunt Mama's room by the odor of oil in the lamps on the altar, and, at the end of the hallway, the succulent smell of the kitchen.'

Gabriel García Márquez, trans. Grossman – *Living to Tell the Tale*, 2003.

By smells we can identify – create – places too: sometimes nice places, sometimes horrid:

> 'Something shattered on the ground inside the tent. A ghastly, gruesome, grisly stinky stench filled the air. "AAAAARGGGGG!" screamed Margaret, gagging. "It's a —STINKBOMB!" "HELP!" shrieked Sour Susan. "STINKBOMB! Help! Help!" '

Francesca Simon – *Horrid Henry's Stinkbomb*, 2002.

INTANGIBLE PLACE IDENTIFIERS 4
noise… or is it music?

'Arglwydd, dyma fi…'

'Gwahoddiad', a Welsh hymn.

Babies cry, children sing, bike bells tinkle… we identify where we are – our place – with sound. If we, as children, are lost and want to be found we shout, '**I'm here!**'.

The sound of gulls cawing, of children shouting, of the sea's surf sucking at the sand or shingle… all these contribute to the identity of a beach as a place. Some might call it music to the ears but the sound of a beach is evocative noise.

We, as children, can identify our place with music too. A child soprano, solo in a cavernous church, fills the space to the vaults with enchantment. A guitarist, toying with busking, gives atmosphere to a whole street, even into its side alleys. The skirl of bagpipes thrills a city.

A clarinettist fills a large sphere of space with the sound of his music.

'Ring a ring a roses; a pocket full of posies.
A-tishoo! a-tishoo! We all fall down.'

You put your left leg in, your left leg out,
In, out, in out, shake it all about.
You do the hokey cokey
And you turn around.
That's what it's all about.'

MAKING PLACES WITH OURSELVES

Our interactions are geometric. Our bodies are innately architectural. The innate geometries of our bodies mean that the ways in which we position ourselves physically in relation to others tend to follow particular patterns. We might stand face-to-face with someone to whom we are talking; or we might sit side-by-side with a friend eating or watching the television. In groups of more than two we might adopt different arrangements. Judging by the places we make as children – whether grown up or not – these standard patterns are factors in our innate sense of architecture. They are part of the metalanguage of architecture. At their most rudimentary they are evident in the ways in which we relate to our friends and family, and to those with whom we are in conflict. But they can be set down in lasting physical frames – architecture – too: in seating arrangements; in the layout of a neighbourhood of houses; or a row of shops along a high street.

MAKING A PLACE WITH OUR FRIENDS
being together

I am the seed and the subject of architecture. I am its perpetrator and its content. Before I make buildings, I make places with myself. Sometimes I make places with my friends – by being in some formation together – or with my enemies – by being in confrontation or conflict. In community is strength. Architecture is possible using nothing but ourselves.

A child reinforces her occupation – and therefore identification of a place – by assembling her friends closely around her, identifying a communal place.

'She piled her books and scrolls (on the great gilded bed), then, crawling across the covers, surrounded herself with them. Rather than read, she touched, savoured their smooth and dry surfaces. Some she held until they became warm as her skin. Then, for no reason she could fathom, she counted them, like a child jealous of her toys.'

R. Scott Bakker – *The Thousandfold Thought: The Prince of Nothing, Book 3,* 2006.

PLACES FORMED OF PEOPLE

We make architecture with ourselves. Sometimes, on special occasions, people build towers out of themselves (right), leaving small children to occupy the most precarious positions.

More often we might find ourselves making more simple and less dangerous architectural formations.

A sports team's huddle creates a communal circle evoking precedents (stone circles and village greens) from the past.

In various parts of Spain, at different times of year, communities compete to erect the tallest and most stable tower with their own bodies. Children, because they are small and light, are delegated to complete the topmost storey.

At the end of a match the winning team might form a pathway of applause – a guard of honour – to salute their opponents.

There are many examples of architectural formations that originate with our own bodies.

Before the wall was built between East and West Berlin (in the 1960s) its line was drawn out in armed troops. Collectively they constituted a wall which was only later built in concrete.

SIDE-BY-SIDE
being together

We place ourselves alongside our friends. We stand, sit or lie side-by-side. We eat next to each other. Our togetherness is readable in our formation – the architecture of our relative positioning. The geometric patterns of such spatial relationships can be manifest, enshrined, in the places we make too.

Partners lie scrupulously parallel on a beach.

Two curly-tops watch television together.

FACE-TO-FACE
being in opposition

Sometimes, playing games or perhaps arguing, we place ourselves face-to-face. Though conversations may be friendly, they do involve 'move' and 'counter move'; first one person says something and then the other offers a riposte.

    Face-to-face is the arrangement of conflict. We sit opposite each other playing chess or other board games. Enemy armies face each other across the battlefield.

'The two forces were about to clash, when the godlike Paris stepped out from the Trojan ranks and offered single combat... but when royal Paris saw that it was Menelaus who had taken up his challenge, his heart failed him completely, and he slipped back into the friendly ranks in terror for his life.'

Opponents in a chess game sit opposite each other, face-to-face, in the spatial arrangement of conflict.

Homer, trans. Rieu – *The Iliad* (c. 700 BCE), 1950.

POLYGONAL GROUPINGS
with as many sides as people

When there are more than two of us, we find different formations that allow us to relate to each other and manifest being together.

Four girls sit together in a cross formation (above); with five, it would be a pentagon. It is so natural – intuitive, an ingrained part of our innate language of architecture – that the girls hardly thought about it. They just sat on the sand facing inwards towards each other. And in doing so they adopted an architectural formation, identifying their own collective place.

' " We have to sit in a circle facing each other", said Dr Beech… "In that way we will all be physically and psychologically connected to each other's thoughts, and the images in our minds will go round and around between us, faster and faster, like a fairground carousel." '

Four girls, without thinking, have settled together in a geometrically regular formation – a four-armed cross. If it had been five of them, or six… they would have formed polygons with equivalent numbers of sides.

Graham Masterton – *Fire Spirit*, 2010.

DISTORTION
by something that's there

Sometimes the formations we make are made more complicated by there being more of us in our group or by the contribution of something that is already there. The five boys above make a collective place, but it is not a regular formation. It is distorted by two of them sitting on a branch.

And this family (right), because their blanket is not big enough for all them to sit facing inwards towards each other, have had to adopt a less conventional formation, with all except one of them facing outwards away from the others. Yet their togetherness is in no way lessened.

Togetherness can be expressed facing inwards (above) or outwards (below).

GEOMETRY OF TENTS
beginnings of urban design

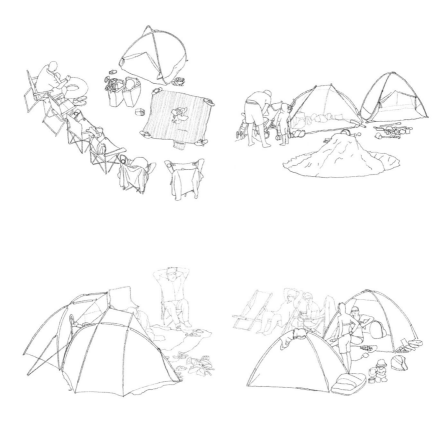

The geometric patterns we make when we situate ourselves in relation to others translate into the patterns we make when we arrange chairs and tents, and into more permanent juxtapositions of buildings. On the beach we tend to place chairs in rows next to each other, maybe in gentle concave curves. Likewise, if we have more than one tent, we might place them alongside each other, next to each other but at right angles (forming a corner), or sometimes opposite each other. The latter two arrangements have the advantage of creating a third space or room in-between – a 'courtyard', two sides of which are defined by the tents.

The possibilities are not limited to the examples shown above. There is more than one way to structure such 'spatial sentences' in the 'language of architecture'.

Like the syntax of language there is a syntax to the ways in which we can arrange our encampments on the beach. This syntax applies equally to more permanent architectural arrangements: in the design of housing and cities. Examples on the beach are evidence of the innate architect in all of us.

*'Children create places for themselves from at least the age of 3
and probably earlier. The earliest forms of places are "found" rather
than built; they are imaginal rather than physical transformations.
Consequently, we cannot know just how early this kind of architecture
begins. I have even observed children as young as 3 years of age
create the familiar form of architecture in which materials are physically
moved and juxtaposed to create new kinds of spaces. Although my
observations have been primarily in the United States, particularly in a
New England town (Hart, 1979), children's architecture appears to be a
universal phenomenon. Perhaps the making of places to be in is one of
a small set of archetypal human behaviors with important survival value
for a culture and developmental advantages for the individual.'*

Roger Hart – 'Children's Participation in Planning and Design: Theory, Research, and Practice', , in
Weinstein and David – *Spaces for Children*, 1987, p. 218.

DEFINING PLACE

Learning to define place for yourself is part of growing up. It is part of becoming
an individual and a step in the progress to independence. Defining place for
yourself is an assertion of presence and the right to space – your own space.
Definition of space is also an assertion of agency, a product of the realisation
that you are able to change your physical world in response to your own needs
and desires. The urge to define place and the capacity for doing so lie at the
core of what it means to be an architect. It is as important to development as is
the acquisition of language.

RIPPLES OF PRESENCE
affecting the world around

The ripples we make when standing in still water are an apt representation of the personal space and presence we each project around ourselves all the time.

    (In this Notebook the focus is on personal spatial presence but, as the quotation below indicates, the 'ripples' of our moral presence can be a powerful metaphor too.)

When a boy stands in calm water his presence is represented in the concentric ripples that emanate from his movements.

'Each time a man stands up for an ideal, or acts to improve the lot of others, or strikes out against injustice, he sends forth a tiny ripple of hope, and crossing each other from a million different centers of energy and daring, those ripples build a current that can sweep down the mightiest walls of oppression and resistance.'

Robert F. Kennedy – Speech at the University of Cape Town, South Africa, 6 June 1966.

RECOGNISING A DEFINED PLACE
puddles

Set in an expansive empty beach, these girls have recognised a shallow puddle of remnant sea water as a place. Its edges are irregular and blend into the sand but nevertheless the water defines a surface distinguished from the general beach. It is not clear what the girls are actually doing in this puddle. Sometimes we are drawn to a defined place (as in the case of the tree on pages 60–61) just because of its being defined, being identifiable as a place amongst an otherwise featureless or confused tract of the world's surface. Places stand out by reason of their definition.

These girls have recognised a place defined by a patch of water left behind by the receding tide.

'Peppa and George love jumping in muddy puddles...'

Neville Astley and Mark Baker – *Muddy Puddles*, 2004.

DEFINED AREAS
arena, stage, prayer mat…

You can relate to place that is defined. An area of ground defined by the edges of a carpet, a platform, a square or circle drawn on a beach or in a field. The definition of the area reinforces your presence; it sits you in a particular place. It can protect and orient you. Defined areas transport; they can be transportable too (below).

My granddaughter sits making daisy chains on the timber deck in her great-grandmother's garden.

'I loved my prayer rug… Wherever I laid it I felt special affection for the patch of ground beneath it and the immediate surroundings, which to me is a clear indication that it was a good prayer rug because it helped me remember that the earth is the creation of God and sacred the same all over. The pattern… was plain: a narrow rectangle with a triangular peak at one end to indicate the qibla.'

Yann Martel – *Life of Pi*, 2003.

TAKING POSSESSION
this is mine

We want space for ourselves. So we take it by asserting boundaries. It becomes our place. Such an assertion of possession might provoke conflict, for which we may or may not be prepared. But the desire to possess our own space, our place, is a powerful one.

We can define our place most simply by drawing a line around it. We do it personally on a beach. Armies and politicians do the same thing at a larger scale, to be recorded on maps.

The boy in the drawing above made a first tentative attempt to define his space amongst the rocks with a feint single line. Reconsidering, he claimed more territory by digging a trench, with consequent rampart of displaced sand, at the mouth of the inlet. The next step would be to build an impenetrable wall.

A boy lays claim to the space contained by an inlet in the rocky cliffs by digging a line – a boundary – across its entrance. For him the line becomes the threshold of his place. For others it is a wall excluding them until they might be invited in.

ASSERTING POSSESSION
keep out!

Before anything else, architecture is about identifying place. This involves the recognition of place and the manipulation of it to suit desired purposes.

    This boy (above) has found and occupied a place on the beach. It is defined by an almost vertical retaining wall at its rear and a spur of natural rock to one side. These form two walls of what can be interpreted as a room. The boy has interpreted it as such and decided to take possession of it. He sits on his deckchair looking out of the room's open side – its 'glass wall' – towards the sun and the sea. He has stored his belongings within the defined space of the room. He has draped his damp towels on the rocky spur to dry. He is 'at home'.

    But the room has a problem.

This boy has found and taken possession of a 'room' suggested by a high retaining wall and a rocky spur. It faces the sea through one of its open sides and catches the sun; but this room has a problem. It is situated near public access onto the beach.

'(Romulus) described a quadrangular figure about the hill, tracing with a plough drawn by a bull and a cow yoked together a continuous furrow designed to receive the foundation of the wall.'

Dionysius of Halicarnassus, trans. Cary – *Roman Antiquities* (1st C. BCE), Book 1:88, 1937.

rocky spur

retaining wall

DON'T CROSS

● access from steps down onto the beach

The boy has become aware that his room does not quite provide him with the exclusivity he desires. It lies at the base of a public access to the beach from the cliff above.

He has clearly experienced discomfort that some people accessing the beach have intruded into what he feels is his place, his personal domain. And so he has firmly drawn a line – a threshold – and made it into a wall by writing emphatically 'DON'T CROSS' along it. (He has even supplemented this asserted barrier with a fishing net.)

The line presents no physical barrier to further intrusion. But few would cross it. The line and instruction have psychological power. The boy's drawn line and its accompanying command have become the third wall of his room.

The boy has exercised his architectural faculties in recognising and occupying the 'room'. Becoming aware of the problem – people inadvertently intruding on his assumed domain – his architectural faculty kicks in again. He 'builds a wall' – in the form of a line supplemented by an instruction (and a fishing net) – to reinforce the definition of his place. (He seems unconcerned that his architectural intervention might be interpreted as rudely assertive.)

BUILDING A BARRIER 1
you are not my friend!

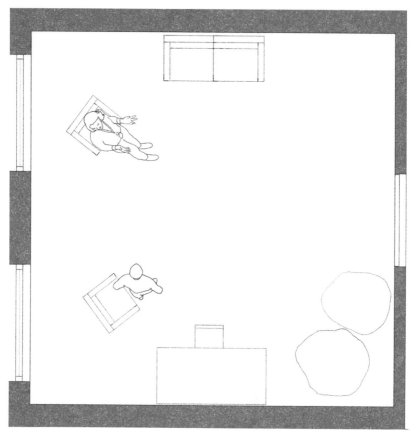

I shall not attempt to analyse this example psychologically. It was reported to me as having happened at a session between a young person and his psychotherapist.

At the beginning of the session the room was laid out as shown above, with its usual arrangement of furniture consisting of two armchairs, a sofa, a table with chair, and a couple of bean bags.

The room provided the enclosed arena for the conversation between the young person and his therapist. Furniture can be a factor in the relationship between people. In the above arrangement the two arm chairs are arranged in 'non-committal' relationship; neither facing each other – in 'opposition' – nor side-by-side – in 'agreement'.

A young man is in a room with his psychotherapist. The furniture of the room is arranged for a conversation; neither in opposition nor with undue intimacy.

ANALYSING ARCHITECTURE NOTEBOOKS

BUILDING A BARRIER 2
or am I uncomfortable with connection?

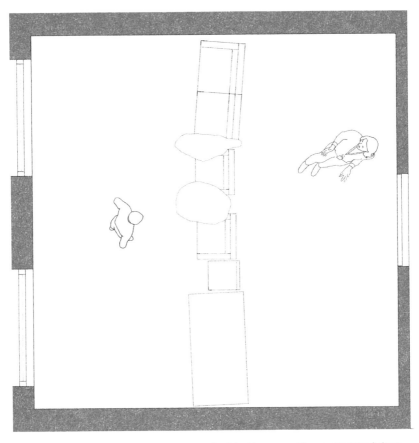

During the session the young person decided he wanted to rearrange the furniture radically. His alternative arrangement is illustrated above. He is on the left; the therapist on the right; with all the room's furniture arranged into a barrier – a barricade – in-between. Having built his defences, he proceeded to fire across the barricade with a pretend gun made from Lego blocks.

It is not clear why the young person chose to confine himself in the half of the room with the windows – sources of light and view – rather than that with the door – the route of escape. But such might be a factor in one's interpretation of what the young person was 'saying' with his architectural act. After all, this was certainly an attempt at communication through the language of architecture.

The young man brings his innate architect into play. He does so in a way that might be interpreted as indicating some aspects of his state of mind. He rearranges all the room's furniture into a barricade between him and his therapist. What does he want to defend himself against? (I am not qualified to guess all the subtleties of what this all means.) Or was it just that he was keen to fix himself in this secure place?

FREE ENTRY
generosity with place

Of course, when you assume control of space –
of a place – it is within your power to can grant
permission to enter as well as to keep people out.
Architecture can be a matter of generosity as well
as acquisition.

    The image above shows a pit dug in the
sand which, because of the level of the tide, is half
full of water. As a place it is like a baptismal font.
The architect has clearly been pleased with what
he has achieved and presumably enjoyed sitting
in its amniotic water before re-emerging into the
world. So much so that he wanted to offer the
same transformative experience to others, free of
charge.

    By signing it, the font's architect seems also
to have wanted to take credit for its creation and for
the magnanimity of making it freely available to all.

*I do not know whether the
boy exiting stage left is the
architect of the baptismal
font or whether he has
just been availing himself
of the opportunity for free
access to it. He may have
just been wandering past.*

LIVING ON A GAME BOARD
spatial rules

Our surroundings, usually for the common good, are organised into defined areas. Our pavements can be similar to the board layout of a game with spatial rules laid down in white lines – rules we are encouraged, sometimes required by law, to obey. As children we learn about these spatial rules and probably, at times, test what happens when we transgress them.

The architecture of sense is fundamental to architectural intervention. And, in reciprocation, architectural intervention is a matter of making sense. Sense is made for us, for example, by the layout of white lines on our streets and pavements. They set down the spatial rules for moving around.

This girl may not be obeying the 'road markings' on this mainly pedestrian promenade by the sea, but she has less choice as to whether she must submit to the control over movement effected by the railings and walls.

When we travel to places where there are no white lines to govern our movements and those of others it feels strange, less safe, strangely unnerving… We like the order imposed by lines of demarcation.

ARCHITECTURE IS ABOUT DEFINING AREAS
about identifying place and organising space

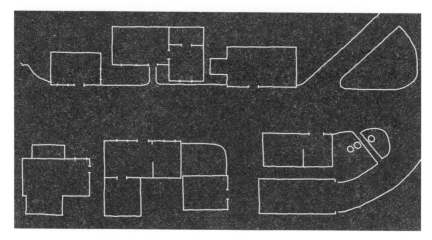

In the film *Dogville* (Lars von Trier, 2003) the town in which it is set, rather than being built as realistic buildings, is defined by white lines on a black ground (above) like chalk drawings on a blackboard. As in a board game, these provide the spatial rules for the drama.

The drawing below shows beach camps for two friendly families. The children have allocated space for each family within a niche in the rocks by outlining them with trenches – like neighbouring houses with adjacent front doors. Maybe the families are neighbours at home too.

IT'S ALL MINE
consignment to 'no place'

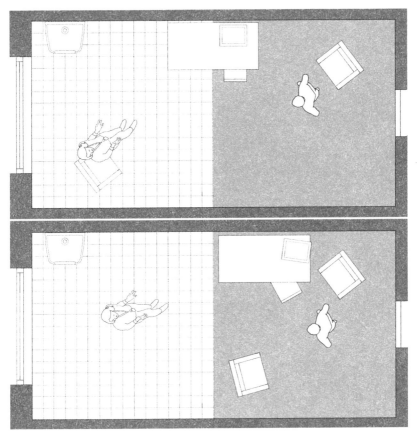

'He moved the furniture around the room, leaving only a small patch of the room with nothing in it for me. He made a border between my bare side of the room and his. He tried to forbid me from even leaning on the table.' Anonymised psychiatric report.

On pages 98–9 I illustrated an instance where a young person built a barrier between himself and his psychotherapist. The two drawings above illustrate another such interaction expressed architecturally. It happened in a different room. The floor was divided into two: half tiled, half carpeted. In a temper the young person pulled all the moveable furniture on to 'his', carpeted, portion of the room, leaving the therapist stranded on the tiles. Presumably this act was a defiant assertion, expressed architecturally, that it was he, not her, that was in control.

In a confrontation with his therapist a young person appropriates all the room's furniture for himself by pulling it across a threshold between tiled and carpeted floor. In this 'chess game' he has taken all his 'opponent's' pieces. The therapist is left in a desert of tiles – in 'no place'.

INHABITATION IS ITSELF A GAME
of identifying place and organising space

If we define a game as a pattern of behaviour that follows (or breaks) a common rule system – rather than as some inconsequential recreation – then all inhabitation may be interpreted as a game.

In the drawing above the resident family have found and allocated places for themselves and all their belongings. The arrangement signifies relationships too.

In my study at home (right) everything is arranged (not very tidily) for my 'game' of writing books and drawing. Computer, screens, scanner, books… all are arranged to frame the moves.

My study (below) is the court within which I play the game of writing books.

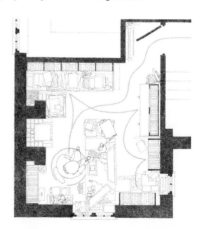

ANALYSING ARCHITECTURE NOTEBOOKS

'One of the most important characters of play was its spatial separation from ordinary life. A closed space is marked out for it either materially or ideally, hedged off from the everyday surroundings. Inside this space the play proceeds, inside it the rules obtain. Now the marking out of some sacred spot is also the primary characteristic of every sacred act. This requirement of isolation for ritual, including magic and law, is much more than merely spatial and temporal. Nearly all rites of consecration and initiation entail a certain artificial seclusion for the performers and those to be initiated. Whenever it is a question of taking a vow or being received into an Order or confraternity, or of oaths and secret societies, in one way or another there is always such a delimitation of room for play. The magician, the augur, the sacrificer begins his work by circumscribing his sacred space. Sacrament and mystery presuppose a hallowed spot. Formally speaking there is no distinction whatever between marking out a space for a sacred purpose and marking it out for purposes of sheer play. The turf, the tennis court, the chessboard and pavement-hopscotch cannot formally be distinguished from the temple or the magic circle.'

Johan Huizinga – *Homo Ludens* (1944, 1950), 1955, p.19–20.

PLACES FOR GAMES

Many aspects of life may be comparable to games, and the places for them organised like courts or pitches. But we make places for actual sports and games too. Some are elaborate. But the ones we make on the flat sands of a beach or on the lawns of our gardens and yards are usually simple. They often start with the definition of an area of ground, distinguishing a playing area from the general outside – a 'sacred space' as Huizinga suggests (see quotation above). When a ball or a person goes outside of that area – into the 'nowhere' outside – it becomes dead and a point is lost. The defined area is often divided into two face-to-face territories in opposition and conflict. Sometimes a net or rope divides the two opponent areas. Sometimes those antagonists' realms focus at their ends on a goal which they or their teams must attack and try to breach with the ball. The focus of the action is concentrated within the defined and sacred arena.

A SIMPLE BALL COURT
the sacred realm of play

We do it almost thoughtlessly when we are on the beach and want to play a ball game: but laying out a pitch or court – for whatever game – is the incantation of a magic spell by inscription in the sand. The magic conjures up a place with rules, rules expressed by lines; spatial rules that define places and set the frame within which the game is played. An inside – the arena for the ceremonial interaction – is distinguished from the general outside – non-place. A ball's bounce in relation to a boundary line determines whether it is 'IN' or 'OUT'. Often, in straightforward or more complex ways, two individuals or teams are placed in opposition to each other, for a contest. The pitch, with its defined areas, is the architecture (or at least part of the architecture) of the game; its 'receptacle of becoming', its chora.

The architecture of a cricket pitch (below) places teams in opposition to each other in more complex ways than that of a simple volley-ball or tennis court (above).

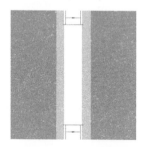

A GAME WITH MORE COMPLEX ARCHITECTURE
beach cricket

On the beach a cricket pitch is reduced to its essentials. The stumps may be no more than some pieces of driftwood or a bucket. The length of the pitch is decided by judgement rather than measured, geared to the age and ability of the players rather than official rules. The surface of the pitch rapidly becomes uneven producing random bounces. The boundary, over which one always wants to score a SIX, might be the lapping surf of the sea, and therefore approach or recede according to whether the tide is ebbing or flowing.

But even in this rudimentary form, those essential elements of a cricket pitch establish its architecture. A complex and special place is created on the sand's blank canvas. And the place frames narratives of unplayable balls, massive hits, acrobatic catches...

These boys, with their father, have established a special place – for the playing of cricket – with just a few simple elements: a wicket for the bowler to aim at; a point for the bowler to bowl from; and the shifting tide as a boundary.

STREET FOOTBALL
economical game architecture

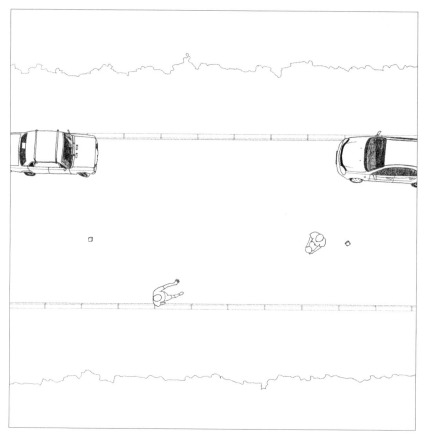

I encountered one of the most economical instances of the rudimentary identification of place for a game in the Turkish city of Iznik. I did not notice it at first. I just saw boys playing football (soccer). Then I saw they had defined their pitch quite precisely but with great economy of means.

All the boys needed to conjure up a complete football pitch was two small stones. With these they managed to define two goals and suggest their goal lines. The touch lines along each side of the pitch were defined by the kerbs. The game was being played in a space between two parked cars. The corners of those cars provided the additional two goal posts required.

And so, with just two stones, the boys had established all the essential elements of their football pitch.

Some boys are playing soccer on a street near their homes. They have created their pitch mainly using things that are there already... plus just two stones, carefully and precisely positioned to create, with the help of parked cars, two goals.

'But lo, the world hath many centres, one for each created being, and about each one it lieth in its own circle. Thou standest but half an ell from me, yet about thee lieth a universe whose centre I am not but thou art.'

Thomas Mann, trans. Lowe-Porter – *Joseph in Egypt* (1936), 1999.

'I think I told you that this good woman was a person of no small note and consequence throughout our whole village and township; – that her fame had spread itself to the very out-edge and circumference of that circle of importance, of which kind every soul living, whether he has a shirt to his back or no, – has one surrounding him; – which said circle, by the way, whenever 'tis said that such a one is of great weight and importance in the world, – I desire may be enlarged or contracted in your worship's fancy, in a compound-ratio of the station, profession, knowledge, abilities, height and depth (measuring both ways) of the personage brought before you.'

Laurence Sterne – *Tristram Shandy* (1759), 1983.

CIRCLE

We are constantly negotiating relationships with our physical surroundings. By looking at how, as children, we make places intuitively we can gain insight into the primitive beginnings of place-making and our common language of architecture. One of the most powerful driving forces in this is our deeply seated desire for envelopment as an antidote to abiding agoraphobic caution in our relationship with the world, or at least as a counterpoint to being in the 'great outdoors'. As babies we are embraced; as parents we do the embracing; when we die we are enveloped in coffins and tombs. The desire for envelopment is fundamental to the architecture we make as children, as it is to all architecture. And the most rudimentary form that provides this envelopment is the delineated loop, represented in its pure Platonic form as a geometrically perfect circle. Circles (most often as rough loops rather than geometric figures) are common in the places we make as children. They are popular because of their capacity to contain, to envelope. Such circles seem to emerge from some intuitive impulse.

ENVELOPING 1
swaddled…

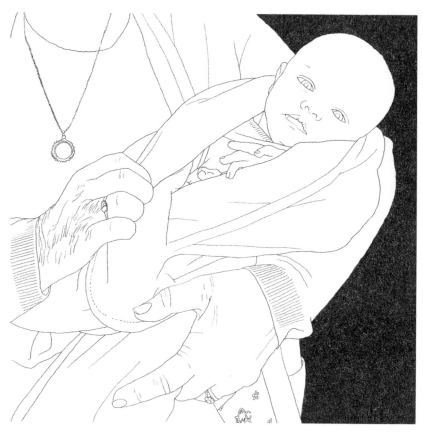

The ubiquitous experience of early human life is being held in the arms of a parent. We are predisposed to hold our babies; and we can only presume that, as babies, we are predisposed to enjoy being held. Our parents and grandparents clothe us and swaddle us in blankets. Such envelopment speaks of love and protection.

When we are not hugging them we place our babies in the encircling comfort of a cradle or cot, a small place with walls, for sleeping in safety. The desire for envelopment is a driving force in architecture. It is fundamental to our psychological security in a threatening world.

We experience physical and psychological comfort in being embraced, enveloped, protected.

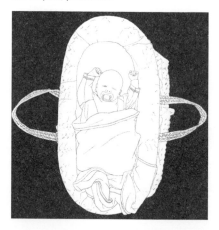

ANALYSING ARCHITECTURE NOTEBOOKS

ENVELOPING 2
encircled...

an ancient burial cist found on the isle of Barra, one of the Outer Hebrides off Scotland

Creatures of all kinds are enveloped in their eggs or wombs (below). We humans envelope our dead in tombs (above).

The circle envelopes. In 'Twilight' (below; 1975) the artist Joan Jonas placed herself inside a hoop, like a foetus or a corpse.

OUTLINE
my straitjacket

‘The immediate place of a thing is neither less nor greater than the thing.’
Aristotle, trans. Hardie and Gaye – *Physics* (350 BCE),
Book IV, Part 4, 1930.

Aristotle (see the quotation above) suggested that an object's place was no more nor less than the space it occupies. Plato, by contrast, referred to something he called the 'chora' or the 'receptacle of becoming'. He seemed to suggest that place might be defined more subtly, including space for life and change in time.

The chalk line that detectives draw around a dead body (right), or the line in the sand the boy has drawn about his sister (above), delineates the Aristotelian concept of place. But to live, the boy's sister needs more space; she needs an arena in which to breathe and move. As do we all.

One day I was walking home. A prankster had aerosoled an outline on the path to suggest it was the place where a dead body had been discovered.

ARENA
my sphere of influence

In *The Ten Most Influential Buildings in History* (2017, page 72) I recounted an event witnessed on a beach. It was ephemeral yet significant in its illustration of the idea that we need more space to live than just that bounded by the outline of our body. It also shows how place-making can play a part in personal interactions and allegiances.

A small group of girls was frolicking across the beach. One carrying a stick stopped suddenly. As she swiftly drew a circle about herself in the sand, she shouted at the others, who had to look back: 'Whoever comes into my circle is my friend'. The other girls paused. (You can imagine the quandaries in their minds.) Then one ran into the circle and hugged the girl with the stick.

As an example of how an act of architecture – drawing a circle – can be an instrument of personal interaction, this ephemeral event is replete with subtlety and complexity. What prompted the action? Was the girl with the stick insecure or seeking to establish/reinforce leadership? What was going through the minds of the other girls while deliberating whether or not to enter the circle? Were they reticent or even rebellious against this attempted assertion of authority? Was it insecurity or genuine friendship that prompted the one girl to enter the circle? Such are the subtle possibilities prompted by rudimentary architecture.

ENVELOPING
individuation

Given our predilection for envelopment, it is to be expected that when we begin to make places for ourselves, we do so by enveloping ourselves actually or metaphorically. As we grow up we assert our individuality more and more. We can do this physically in making places as well as behaviourally in our relationships with others. And one of the simplest and yet most significant ways we can do this physically is by drawing a circle about our presence. This has to be a fundamental architectural impulse. We do it just by being; we project our own personal space as an intangible bubble around our bodies. We also see it in tangible form when, for instance, a child idly draws a circle in the sand around himself almost without thinking, and without realising the profound significance of what he is doing.

A boy is defining his space, his place and his individual identity by drawing a circle about himself in the sand. In this act lies the germ of all domestic architecture. It represents envelopment and protection. The circle manifests and contains his personal aura, but also allows him to project his imagination out into the world around. The circle supplements infinite space with a second defined and more proximate (knowable) horizon.

ANALYSING ARCHITECTURE NOTEBOOKS

'Visible and mobile, my body is a thing among things; it's caught in the fabric of the world, and its cohesion is that of a thing. But, because it moves itself and sees, it holds things in a circle around itself.'

Maurice Merleau-Ponty – 'Eye and Mind' (1961), 1993.

The achieved circle provides psychological security based in grounding and the delineation of a boundary.

In the quotation below, Gilles Deleuze and Félix Guattari (below) hint at an agoraphobia that lies at the core of our relationship with the world in which we find ourselves:

'A child in the dark, gripped with fear, comforts himself by singing under his breath. He walks and halts to his song. Lost, he takes shelter, or orients himself with his little song as best he can. The song is like a rough sketch of a calming and stabilizing, calm and stable, center in the heart of chaos. Perhaps the child skips as he sings, hastens or slows his pace. But the song itself already has a skip; it jumps from chaos to the beginnings of order in chaos and is in danger of breaking apart at any moment. There is always sonority in Ariadne's thread. Now we are at home. But home does not pre-exist: it was necessary to draw a circle around that uncertain and fragile center, to organize a limited space... The forces of chaos are kept outside as much as possible, and the interior space protects the germinal forces of a task to fulfil or a deed to do.'

Gilles Deleuze and Félix Guattari, trans. Massumi – '1837: Of the Refrain', in *A Thousand Plateaus: Capitalism and Schizophrenia* (1987), 2004.

THE MAGIC CIRCLE 1
distinguishing a place

A circle drawn on a beach has a power of its own.

The surface of a pristine beach is undifferentiated. All parts are much the same. There are areas nearer to the water but otherwise it is a blank canvas.

But if you draw a circle on that pristine beach you alter it fundamentally. You have literally changed the world, if in only a small way.

The circle identifies a place where previously there was none. Such a simple circle has a claim to be the most rudimentary form of architecture.

The circle suggests powers of inclusion and exclusion. Though it will not, you feel it might resist the oncoming tide. Walking across the beach you would probably avoid stepping through the circle (unless you did not notice it). You would recognise it as a place – perhaps belonging to someone – and politeness (or fear) would probably persuade you not to intrude or prick its bubble of magic.

A circle drawn on the ground is a simple but powerful thing. No wonder we might call it a magic circle. Its magic is the seed of all architecture.

THE MAGIC CIRCLE 2
the power of a threshold

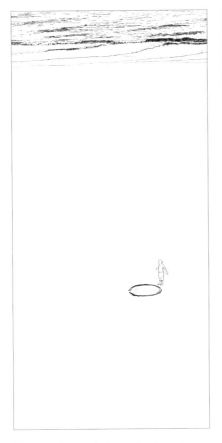

Discovering a circle on the beach, we, as children, hesitate. What does the circle mean? What place does it identify? Does it define a place of danger (where sand is quick or a bomb is buried)? The circle was drawn by someone else; so presumably the place defined 'belongs' to them in some way. I will get no answers to these questions, so maybe I should just walk on, tracing a safe path around the circle's perimeter.

But perhaps, with boldness, I could conquer my trepidation and, holding my breath, cross the circle's threshold to enter it.

I no doubt experience a slight thrill as I do. After all I do not know what might happen when I cross the line. Maybe someone will shout at me or a flash of lightning will strike. Shall I disappear into some parallel world?

But no. There was no threat or danger. And now, in occupying this defined place, I am its lord: it is mine. I have taken possession of the magic circle and it reinforces my status. (Even so, someone might return to claim their territory, shouting, 'Oi! That's my circle! Gerrout!' None of these things would occur on the blank beach. Such things a mere circle may provoke.)

BEING PUT INTO A PLACE
a protective cocoon for a child

One of the abiding realisations of our gradually awakening consciousness of being in the world must be the sense of repeatedly being *put into* a place: into the arms of a grandmother; into a cot; into a pram; into a high chair; into a car seat… The experience of being put into a place is a facet of being cared for, protected, cherished. It is like being placed, temporarily – as if to lessen the abrupt shock of finding ourselves out in the world – back into our egg or womb.

This mother has embraced her child in the cocoon of a sand fortress, which stands as protection against the gently encroaching waves.

'*Pilon got up and drew a big circle around the whole place, and he was inside when he closed the circle. "Let no evil thing cross this line, in the Name of the Most Holy Jesus", he chanted… Then he sat down again. Both he and Big Joe felt better. They could hear the muffled footsteps of the weary wandering ghosts; they could see the little lights that glowed from the transparent forms as they walked by; but their protecting line was impregnable. Nothing bad from this world or from any other would cross into the circle.*'

John Steinbeck – *Tortilla Flat* (1935), 1997.

A REFUGE AGAINST THE SEA
a fortress against fate

A circle can be the embodiment of collective cohesion, of brother- and sisterhood. It can express the unity of a family or the camaraderie of a group of friends.

In the above example three brothers have enjoyed making a fort composed of two concentric sand walls. They are clearly aware, at a subliminal level (it is obvious), that their fort has an inside set against the great outside of the beach and ocean. As the tide approaches they see the inside of their fort as a refuge against the inevitable; and so they entreat the smallest brother to come inside before it is too late.

Of course the sea will win. But this small episode is another example illustrating the social and psychological power of rudimentary architecture.

Older boys encourage their youngest brother to come into the 'safety' of their fortress against the approaching sea. This ephemeral episode is a small but affecting architectural poem, an illustration of how places play their part in relationships.

DEFYING ETERNAL FORCES
against the remorseless tide

Our efforts may fail in the face of the irresistible force of the sea. But, as children, we enjoy attempting resistance. We build forts as defence against the tide but we also enjoy watching our efforts being gradually washed away. This architecture is not about asserting human dominion over the physical world but recognising, in an innately stoical and amused way, that there are, in the universe, more powerful forces than us at work. Building such a fortress is like including ourselves in a joke, the punchline of which is that our efforts to resist universal forces are futile.

A son and father contemplate, philosophically, the incoming tide that will inevitably engulf their fort.

'Roll on, remorseless tide! My rapture was inexplicable… The swell that gladdened my ears and frightened my soul had eight thousand miles of Pacific behind it.'

Zane Grey – *Tales of Fishing Virgin Seas* (1925), 2000.

DEFYING TIME
against the going down of the sun

We might tend to think of these beach constructions as imitations of architecture proper: fortresses, castles, houses... But they are even more primal; they are instances of primitive rudimentary architecture, driven by our innate capacity for place-making.

'The place had a stone circle – a Gilgal – which marked it as a sanctuary, and here young Eliphaz, the highway-robber, durst not have troubled him. In the centre of the Gilgal a peculiar stone was set upright, coal black and cone-shaped – obviously fallen from heaven, and possessing heavenly powers. Its form suggested the organ of generation, therefore Jacob piously saluted it with lifted eyes and hands and felt greatly strengthened thereby.'

Despite this boy's best efforts, his fort is doomed... caught between the rising tide and the lengthening evening shadows.

Thomas Mann, trans. Lowe-Porter – *Joseph and His Brothers* (1933), 1999.

CIRCLES CONTAINING ENIGMATIC POWER
the numinous circle

Sometimes we, as children, make or build (or draw) things that we do not ourselves understand. We do them in a sort of mindless state and then wonder what we have done. In drawing it would be called doodling. We do it in the sand on the beach too. Sometimes we produce enigmatic circles like the one above. What does it mean? It certainly resembles, in form, a prehistoric stone circle.

With no knowledge of their prehistoric precedents, sometimes the places we make as children resemble ancient sacred sites.

'When I began drawing the mandalas, however, I saw that everything, all the paths I had been following, all the steps I had taken, were leading back to a single point – namely, to the mid-point. It became increasingly plain to me that the mandala is the center. It is the exponent of all paths. It is the path to the center, to individuation.'

C.G. Jung, trans. Winston and Winston – *Memories, Dreams, Reflections* (1963), 1977.

CIRCLES OF MEMORY AND PROMISE
hearth and ritual ground

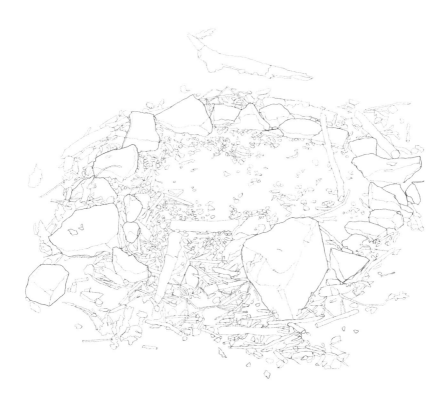

The circle of stones framing the flames of a woodland camp fire persists long after the embers have gone cold and been dampened by the rain. The circle of stones has been the quintessential hearth since the earliest times of human fire building. It defines and kerbs a place. An encounter with an old circular hearth in the woods provokes in our imagination the scene of a similarly circular group of friends sitting around the fire talking. The circular hearth is redolent document of a social event.

We would never stand in the centre of the dead hearth; it is the place of the fire; it is the heart of a social gathering. It is sacred.

'Clearing away brings forth the free, the openness for man's settling and dwelling.'

A flattened circle in the grass, prepared by elders for a boy's ritual circumcision, persists after the ceremony is over – an architectural memory of a significant event.

Martin Heidegger, trans. Seibert – 'Art and Space' (1973), 1997.

A REFUGE AGAINST MORE THAN THE SEA?
a bastion against attack

Traditionally, 1930s German holiday-makers built elaborate sand fortresses on the beaches of the Baltic Sea. Postcards (right) show beaches filled with hundreds of such castles, each the domain of a particular family or group of friends. Some images are accompanied by appropriate verses.

'Wir bauten uns einen Festung
Den feindlichen Wellen zum Trutz.
Nun mögen sie brausen u. toben
Wir sitzen in gutem Schutz.

'Die bunten Fahnen und Wimpel
Sie wehen im Sonnenglanz.
Wir sind vergnügt und singen:
Heil dir im Siegerkranz.'

'We built ourselves a fortress
The enemy waves to defy.
Now they may roar and rage
We sit in good protection.

'The colourful flags and pennants
They blow in the sunshine.
We are happy and sing:
Hail to you in the victor's wreath.'

ANALYSING ARCHITECTURE NOTEBOOKS

MAGICAL PROTECTION
stay there!

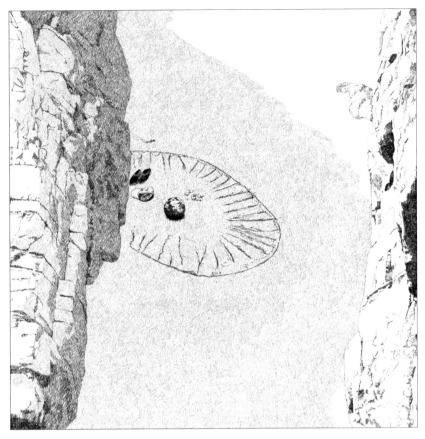

A girl wants to go for a swim. But what should she do with her belongings? How can she keep her treasure safe? She runs behind a rock and places her shoes, hat, ball and some shells in its shadow. She starts to run back towards the sea. But stops; and returns to draw a line in a loop around the treasure. She starts again for the sea, but again stops. She comes back... to add teeth to that protective loop.

And so, with what powers does the girl believe her line and its teeth are invested? Is it to repel potential thieves? Or is it to stop her treasure wandering of its own accord? The teeth point inwards, prodding the treasure to keep it in the place she has put it. Or do they represent the teeth of a mantrap, ready to bite the arm or leg of any intruder? Perhaps all these things?

A girl has protected her treasure with a line. It says – in the language of architecture – that these things are not lost, they belong to someone: 'do not steal them!'.

Are the stones of prehistoric stone circles the equivalent of this girl's rapidly drawn teeth, investing the protective circle with reinforced and threatening strength; strength to protect but also to contain and keep in place?

DEFINING THE PLACE OF A FAMILY
we are all together

As children we might do the same thing with our family as the girl did with her treasure. We might draw a line, or even dig a trench around it to define its place. But perhaps, like the girl's protective line, such a trench says more. Does the architect-child want to celebrate its family's unity. Or is the trench born more of insecurity? Is the line an attempt to strengthen the family's mutual bond? Does the child worry that the bond is not strong?

Why do we as children, or even as adults, draw enclosing and protective circles about our family's encampment on a beach?

'He decided a long time ago "to draw as it were around my desk and chair an imaginary circle. What goes on within the circle I'm totally and completely 100 per cent responsible for. What occurs outside that (reviews and whatnot) there's not much I can do about. The sooner I can get back into my circle the happier I am." '

Robert Harris, quoted in Catherine Nixey – 'Robert Harris: I'd be put off by the words "Booker winner" on the front', in *The Times* (Review Section), 16 September 2017.

REINFORCING FAMILY; PROTECTING THE FORT
do not break apart

One thing is certain in this example. The girl with the plank is intent on reinforcing a place – the place of her family. She has drawn at least four magical circles in a spiral about its encampment; plus a special circle around her bucket.

In medieval times, fortress builders erected layers of protective walls and moats, concentrically arranged in circles or rectangles around the castle's core – its keep. Breaching one line of defence would merely leave attackers facing another.

This sort of employment of spatial language is neither discovered nor invented. It is deep-seated in our innate capacity for architecture. What is said is secondary to the fact that it says something. Architecture communicates in a (mostly) tacit but nevertheless powerful way.

Why might we draw multiple lines? Is doing so the architectural equivalent of a magical incantation, a ritual strengthening of the place and hence of the family that occupies that place? Or is it just fun?

CIRCLE AS VERB
quarantine or shrine?

My wife once asked me to buy a particular Sunday
newspaper, a paper about whose politics I had
reservations. So, as a joke, when I brought it home
I placed it on the kitchen table and encircled it with
a loop of string to contain its 'evil' (below). It struck
me that this is what people have been doing with
circles since time immemorial. It is also something
that we do as children. We use enclosing circles as
'verbs'. We use them to do (to contain) things.

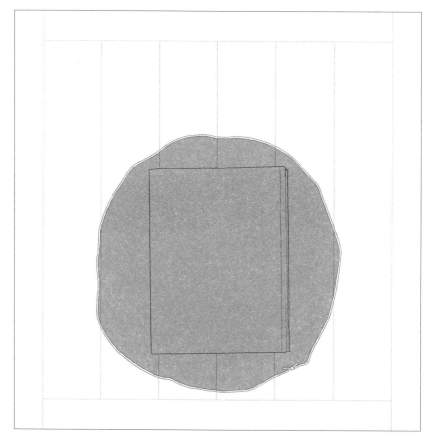

The place might have different relationships with
the surrounding world mediated by the string as an
instrument – the architectural equivalent of a 'doing
word'. Even though the power of the circle is self-evident,
the precise meaning of the place might be private to the
perpetrator of the circle. It this case I, jokingly, encircled
the newspaper to contain its 'evil' – political attitudes not
in accord with mine.

'A circle had been spotted on the corner... In its centre lay a pocket English-Spanish dictionary... A uniformed policeman was already there, guarding the blue chalk circle as if were the holy shroud.'

Fred Vargas, trans. Siân Reynolds – *The Chalk Circle Man* (1991), 2009.

If I had, by contrast, been a devotee of the principles of that newspaper, I could just as well have enclosed it in a circle as a mark of respect, singling it out from the ordinary world as of transcendent worth. In such a situation the circle would become a shrine, and I might have elaborated it with a pair of candlesticks, symbols of light, insight... As children we use circles in this way too, to identify the places of special things.

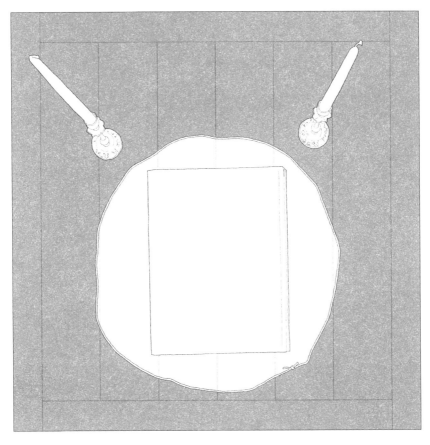

Equally, the circle might be an instrument of celebration. I might have contained the newspaper within the identified place as a mark of respect, of recognition that it deserved its own special realm separate from the ordinary. In this case I might have elaborated the architecture of the place with some symbol – sentinels, a garland of flowers, candlesticks whose light would reinforce the place with their own circle of illumination.

BUBBLE OF PRESENCE
children make it real

1

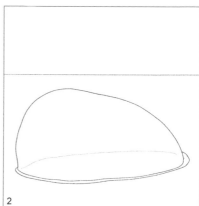

2

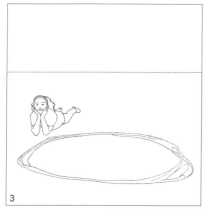

3

4

Play-slime can provide a literal illustration of our desire as children to inhabit bubbles. This glutinous substance may be played with in various ways. One is to stretch it into a thin sheet and, allowing it to collect air (1), drop its edges to the floor so it forms a giant bubble (2).

There is a YouTube video called 'TIANA'S GIANT SLIME BUBBLE!!'. It shows a group of friends making large slime bubbles on the floor. One part of the video powerfully illustrates how we intuitively identify with the place defined by the bubble.

The bubbles slime makes are not stable, nor do they last long. They burst easily leaving a ring of slime on the floor (3). When this happens in the YouTube video, one of the girls almost instantly sees the ring of slime on the floor as a place and quickly jumps into it (4). Playfully smiling, she takes possession of it. It becomes her place.

The girl realises that it would be interesting not only to occupy the remnant slime circle on the floor but to be actually inside the bubble. So she organises her friends to create a bubble over one of them (5).

5

The bubble around one of the girls becomes a tangible manifestation of the bubble of space implied around the boy on the beach (page 115) by the looping line he has drawn around himself in the sand.

The slime economically but impractically (in the sense of providing real protection) replicates the bubbles of space that all huts, igloos, tents, rooms, buildings… create about us, our lives and the things we do. This most primitive architectural idea has had to wait for a modern material to be manifest in its most direct (if useless) form.

It is fun when the bubble bursts too!

CIRCLE OF UNWANTED ATTENTION
'Twigloo'

section

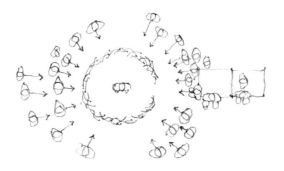

plan

Sometimes architecture tutors ask students to make places in their studios. Once, in the Dundee school, a group of students built a dome out of twigs and branches. We dubbed it the 'Twigloo' (above, in section and plan).

    We singled out one student and made him go inside the Twigloo. He felt very uncomfortable being the centre of attention, with everyone looking at him isolated in the construction, like a defendant in the dock of a courtroom or a prisoner in the medieval stocks.

    Sometimes, being in a circle of attention can be discomforting. It can make you self-conscious and nervous. The Twigloo's construction may have offered some (slight) physical protection but this was outweighed by the psychological vulnerability it provoked.

With the Twigloo, the group of students had made a bubble of presence in physical form. Being inside, singled out from the crowd, was uncomfortable.

CIRCLE OF PROTECTION
Masai hunting camp

section

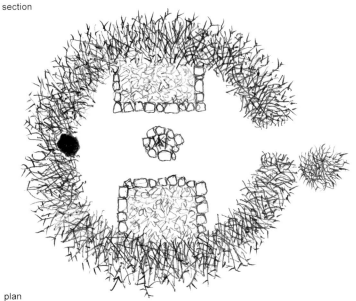

plan

Masai hunters protect themselves at night with their own 'Twigloos' of spikey branches to keep out marauding animals. The hunters build them under the overarching protection of place-identifying trees.

A Masai hunting encampment is a circle of protection against the hunters becoming the hunted.

CIRCLE OF DEFENCE
circle the wagons…

'Fire Thunder speaks: "It was very bad. There is a wide flat prairie with hills around it, and in the middle of this the Wasichus had put the boxes of their wagons in a circle, so that they could keep their mules there at night. There were not many Wasichus, but they were lying behind the boxes and they shot faster than they ever shot at us before… Our ponies were afraid of the ring of fire the guns of the Wasichus made… We left our horses in a gulch and charged on foot, but it was like green grass withering in a fire. So we picked up our wounded and went away. I do not know how many of our people were killed, but there were very many. It was bad." '

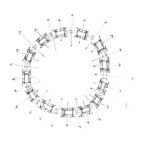

John G. Neihardt – *Black Elk Speaks* (1932), 1979.

Sometimes the places we make, as children on the beach, have the feeling of being fortresses. What do we build them to defend against? We like to be clear about what territory is ours (below).

A father (below) seems to be keeping a lookout for threats to his family's fortress.

CIRCLE OF CONFINEMENT
Primo Levi

In the story 'Titanium', one of his *Periodic Table*, Primo Levi provides an anecdote that illustrates the power of a circle to contain. A little girl will not cross the threshold until given permission and, even then, not until the circle's perimeter line has been erased to break the magic.

'The painted closet was so white that in comparison all the rest of the kitchen looked yellow and dirty. Maria decided there was nothing wrong in going to look at it up close, only look, without touching. But as she was approaching on tiptoe an unexpected and terrible thing happened: the man turned, and in two steps was beside her; he took out of his pocket a white chalk and drew a circle on the floor around Maria. Then he said, "You must stay in there." After which he struck a match, lit his pipe, making many strange grimaces with his mouth, and resumed painting the cupboard. Maria sat on her heels and considered the circle for a long time and attentively; but she became convinced that there was no way out. She tried to rub it at one spot with her finger and saw that the chalk line actually disappeared; but she understood very well that the man would not have regarded that system as valid. The circle was evidently magical. Maria sat on the floor silent and quiet; every so often she tried to reach far enough to touch the circle with the tips of her feet and leaned forward so far that she almost lost her balance, but she soon realized that there was still a good hand's breadth before she could reach the closet or the wall with her fingers. So she just sat there and watched as gradually the cupboard, chairs, and table also became white and beautiful. After a very long time the man put down his brush and paint pot and took the newspaper boat off his head, and then you could see he had hair like all other men. And then he went out by the balcony and Maria heard him rummaging around and tramping up and down in the next room. Maria began to call, "Mister!" – first in a low voice, then louder, but not too loud because at bottom she was afraid the man might hear. Finally the man returned to the kitchen. Maria asked, "Mister, can I come out now?" The man looked down at Maria in the circle, laughed loudly, and said many things that were incomprehensible, but he didn't seem angry. At last he said, "Yes, of course, now you can come out". Maria looked at him perplexed and did not move; then the man picked up a rag and wiped away the circle very carefully, to undo the enchantment. When the circle had disappeared, Maria got up and left, skipping and she felt very happy and satisfied.'

Primo Levi, trans. Rosenthal – 'Titanium', in *The Periodic Table*, 1975.

FIXING LOVE
protective shrine

Sometimes circles are square or rectangular. Even so their architectural purpose and effect remain the same – to identify place.

The boy above seems to be making a special place – with the plan of a temple (including a doorway oriented to the sea) – for his girlfriend. The places we make are often motivated by a desire to love and cherish: 'with this (square) Ring I thee wed...'.

Protective places can be made in many different ways, even just by creating a patch of shadow with an umbrella (right). All constitute architecture.

A ball-boy creates a protective area of shade to protect the super-star tennis player (below).

BATTLE GROUND
throwing out

Circles (circular and square) can be arenas for conflict too. The ring defines the territory under dispute.

Whether for a game of marbles or Sumo, the circle is the arena of conflict, with expulsion meaning defeat.

Gangs of Glenrothes (Scotland) choose the space under a bridge at the joint boundary of their respective territories for their battles.

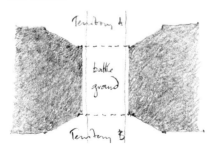

PERFORMANCE CIRCLE 1
drawing attention to oneself

On page 66 I described the way in which a clown can create a stage merely with his performance. We recognise when ephemeral performance places are made more permanent in architectural form too. Here a cockpit clearly defines a circle of space intended originally for the performance of mortal combat between cockerels. It is surrounded by sitting steps for the audience.

We project ourselves into such architecturally defined bubbles of space in our imaginations and then by actually occupying them... and proceed to perform.

Crossing the threshold of such a performance area we feel obliged to put on an act. Sitting on a step we feel obliged to watch! The circle becomes an instrument of interaction, inter-relationship.

When we find a bubble of space concretised in architectural form for the purpose of performance, we feel obliged to perform in it or to spectate. As children, we recognise its identity and respond accordingly.

The circular performance place illustrated above was originally used for the now illegal sport of cock-fighting. It has been rebuilt, and used for less bloody performances, at the St Fagans National Museum of History near Cardiff in South Wales.

PERFORMANCE PLACE 2
the open circle (Peter Brook)

In the book *The Open Circle*, the theatre director Peter Brook describes performance circles installed in his Parisian theatre, Bouffes du Nord. In doing so he identifies some of the powers of a circle to identify place, powers we seem, through our innate capacity for architecture, to understand intuitively. These include the power to identify place and to be associated with (to frame) the identity of its inhabitants. Brook also hints at the power of a sphere of firelight.

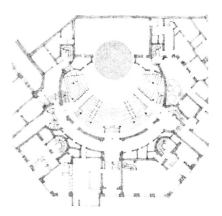

'The (Ik) villagers created their space by spreading dried moss on to a circular zone on the stage... The mossy circle changed the space in two important ways: it delimited an acting area which could mean something quite different when one was inside as opposed to outside, and it also brought a specific material representation, a sense of the parched vegetation of Uganda, into the space of the Bouffes. Its shape and size with respect to the architecture played on a delicate set of balances: in the ellipsoidal arena of the Bouffes a circle is a neutral form, not setting a specific counterpoint with the shape of the building. At around 8 metres in diameter, the circle fitted the width of the proscenium opening, and left a blank zone before the first row of cushion seats. The audience therefore understood it as an "acting area" apart from their own space, but also as representing a specific place, the Ik's settlement, with a "real" material – as "real" as the scarred wall of the theatre up to which it crept. Its circular form also served to avoid a literal description of the Ik's space: it was understood as a general, self-contained sign of "village", left up to the actors to interpret... A fire was lit on stage during The Ik *(a campfire used to cook a rabbit), and this was something that would reappear in* La Tragédie de Carmen *and* The Mahabharata *with considerable force... the fire was grounded, given context, by our awareness that this element, out of control, had touched the actual walls of the building. When the few surviving Ik were forcibly dispatched to different territories at the end of the play, the actors cleared the stage, stuffing the moss back into canvas sacks and taking it off with them. The space reverted to the Bouffes du Nord; we became implicated in the disappearance of the Ik.'*

A circle of moss identifies a specific narrative space in the context of the theatre. It is the village of the Ik. And when the Ik disappear, the circle disappears too.

Peter Brook, in Andrew Todd and Jean-Guy Lecat – *The Open Circle*, 2003.

SOCIAL CIRCLE
a parliament

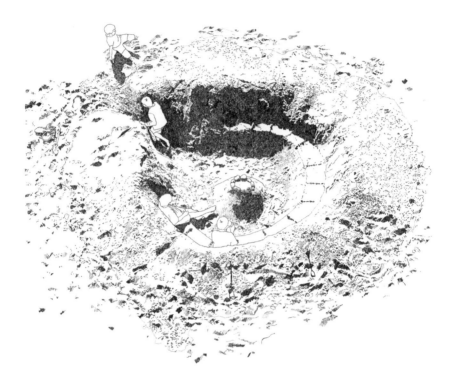

This is one of the most accomplished works of architecture I have seen on a beach. It is also on page 52, as an example of van der Laan's observation that we take from the land to divide up space. But it is also a prime example of the way architecture can frame a social circle. These boys have built for themselves a 'council chamber', a 'chapter house' where they can sit, without hierarchy, and talk. They have included a central focus too – a mound, topped with a ring of stones, which acts as an 'altar' and an axis mundi. The entrance, as one would expect, is oriented to the infinite ocean.

The 'council chamber' the boys have built is identical in its underlying form to a medieval monastic chapter house.

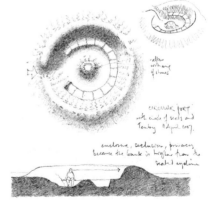

SOCIAL CIRCLES
communal circles

We make social circles when we go to music festivals too. At first sight the drawing above seems to show a higgledy-piggledy distribution of tents (at the 2018 Reading Festival). But on closer inspection you can see that the general mess resolves into a number of focal points where festival goers are sitting around in circles defined by their tents. Some of these have camp-fires at their centres.

There seem to be intuitive architectural rules governing such settlements. Some primitive settlements have similar layouts, with pathways threading between the encampments.

This mass of tents is not arranged randomly. Many of them encircle shared spaces as social circles. There is a general interplay – as the layout evolves with new arrivals – between the desire of a group of friends to make their own circle up against those that are already established. This has been termed an 'organic' mechanism for planning settlements. It was the way rural villages grew in past times, even into large cities. Nowadays, except in music festivals, we tend to want settlements fully planned before they are built.

GOING ROUND IN CIRCLES
rounders or baseball

Lines can be routes of movement – pathways – as well as barriers – walls. As well as being thresholds – lines of demarcation between an inside and the general outside – circles can be lines of movement. The lines followed by the batters in the game of rounders illustrated above trace out a circle that also identifies the place of the game.

As routes, lines can identify place just as strongly as when they are acting as thresholds or boundaries. Often lines on the ground are both. When you walk along a city wall or the parapet of a castle's curtain wall you are also tracing out its boundary. Romulus drew out the boundary of the future city of Rome with a pair of oxen and a plough (see page 97); he killed his brother Remus for crossing it. Some villages annually 'beat' their boundaries to reinforce their power.

The track we trace playing baseball or rounders is a circle of movement.

Though the bases may form the figure of a diamond, the route followed by batters trying to score a home run is more rounded. This becomes evident in the footprints left in the sand.

A CEREMONIAL PATHWAY
a mysterious installation

Sometimes, as children, we trace out routes to follow. These might be tracks for cycling, or clues for treasure hunts. But sometimes, it seems, we lay out ritual pathways for mysterious reasons.

The boys above have created a strange ceremonial pathway from a small circle of movement to a larger one centred on an upright pole. They follow this pathway and then walk clockwise (like the sun) around the pole.

These boys have bemused themselves by building a ceremonial pathway. They follow its ritual route, culminating in processing clockwise around the pole.

See also: *The Ten Most Influential Buildings in History: Architecture's Archetypes,* 2017, p. 28.

TELLING TIME 1
an attempted sun clock

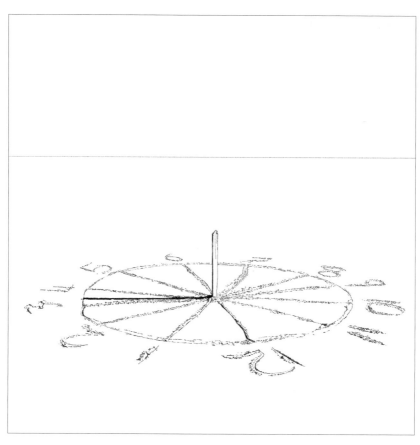

There is an intimate relationship between the circle and time telling. It persists in our circular clock faces.

When I was in primary school we were taught how to measure time using the sun. We used a netball post fixed in the yard and went out each hour to mark the end of its shadow. By doing so we created a sort of clock face. On subsequent days we could tell the time by the sun's shadow. A sundial (right) works in the same way.

Above is a similar device I found left on a beach. A circle has been drawn about a post planted in the sand. Starting from the shadow cast at a known time – say 12.00 noon – this clock maker has divided the circle into twelve equal segments by which he or she thought the time could be told.

You can make a place to tell the time by planting a stick in the ground and watching its shadow move.

TELLING TIME 2
with my own shadow

The architect of the beach sundial opposite possibly made a mistake believing that each segment would be traversed in an hour like on a conventional clock face. But, in a twenty-four hour day, the hands of a clock go through *two* full cycles. On this beach sundial it will take two hours for the shadow to traverse one segment. Thus the time shown in the drawing is about 18.50 or 6.50 p.m.. (The number of hours in a day is of course arbitrary; someone – an architect of time – chose twenty-four many years ago.)

The beach sundial is of no use to tell the time at night or when it is cloudy. It depends on there being sun. But, whether with a stick or yourself, its circle does identify a special place for telling the time.

You could take the place of the stick yourself. You could then tell the time by where your own shadow falls.

TELLING TIME 3
by watching the sun's path

There is another way in which a circle can be a place to tell the time. If you put markers – standing stones for example – in a circle and stand at its centre, you can estimate the time of day by the position of the sun in the sky in relation to those stones. You can also estimate the time of year by the position of the sunrise and the sunset in relation to those same stones. You might position one special stone to mark the position on the horizon where the sun sets on the shortest day of the year – so that you know that from that point the days will get longer – or where it rises on the longest day – so that you know to start preparing for autumn and a colder season.

The circle's association with telling the time is, in its prehistoric origins, architectural.

In this method, stars too would work.

Doorways manifest sight-lines. The doorway of the Maeshowe burial chamber on Orkney is oriented to the setting sun on the shortest day of the year.

ANALYSING ARCHITECTURE NOTEBOOKS

'(Children) seldom worry if an ad hoc collection of cardboard boxes and blankets resembles something specific. In fact, what is so nice about a box is that at one time it can be a jail, the next time a palace, and later a rocket ship or the inside of a whale.'

Leland G. Shaw – 'Designing Playgrounds for Able and Disabled Children', in
Weinstein and David, 1987, p. 204.

'It's NOT NOT NOT NOT a box!'

Antoinette Portis – *Not a Box*, 2006.

'The boxcars, twelve of them, stood end-to-end on a little flat beside the stream. There were two rows of six each, the wheels removed. Up to the big sliding doors slatted planks ran for cat-walks. They made good houses, water-tight and draftless, room for twenty-four families, one family in each end of each car.'

John Steinbeck – *Grapes of Wrath* (1939), 2002.

BOX

In one sense a box might be seen as a ready-made piece of architecture. A box is, by definition, a container, a frame of space. Its purpose is to have things put into it, which includes our possessions but might also include ourselves. Much comment is made about the potential of a box for narrative play (see the top two quotations above) but maybe we have a more visceral relationship with boxes. Maybe the stories we project onto boxes are all born of our innate claustrophilia, our liking for being enclosed, hugged, protected… Before it becomes a boat or space-craft, a box offers the psychological comfort of envelopment; it appeals to our phenomenological appreciation of the 'female'* aspect of architecture: its offer of maternal refuge.

* See pages 37–42 of the *Metaphor* Notebook.

PUTTING OUR SELVES INTO A PLACE
placing something in a box

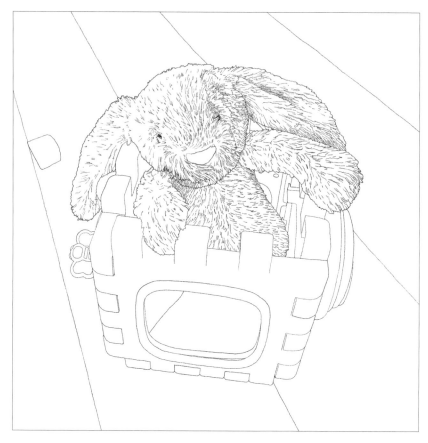

It is no surprise that as children we develop a conscious appreciation of the nature of a place, and imitate our parents' putting us into a place, by putting our vicarious selves – our anthropomorphic toys – into similar places.

One of the most appreciable places we encounter is a box. It is like a room. It is enclosed. Its inside is clearly distinguished from the outside. With a lid its interior is hidden, secret. But even without a lid it is a special place, a place where something, maybe one's self, is clearly contained.

Inside a box is a safe place. A box keeps a thing safe in its place.

As children we can also imagine a box as other things: a house; a boat; a space ship; a castle; a motor car; a fire-engine… But first of all it *is* a box.

The child as mother has put the rabbit into the safe and distinct place offered by a plastic toy box.

An empty cardboard box is a simple toy, open for endless interpretation.

JACK IN A BOX
just being in a box

Being in a box seems to elicit a reflective mood in small children. They are pleased to be there (except when they have had enough and want to get out). It sometimes quietens them. They seem to reflect on the phenomenological experience of being in this defined, and maybe protective, place.

Sometimes a parent will make a box more comfortable for the child by including a blanket or cushion. Sometimes small children are accompanied in their boxes by companion toys or perhaps the family cat.

Whatever the situation, the experience of being in a box is, in itself – with no necessary associated narrative – a powerful and affecting experience.

What would be the equivalent experience for an adult, for whom a packing box is too small? The examples are numerous: a cosy room; a potting shed; a jacuzzi; a meditation chamber; a rowing boat; a study or personal library… From box upwards in scale, all constitute architecture.

Quite independently, at different times in different places, two of my grandchildren have enjoyed, and been bemused by, the experience of sitting in a box.

It is not that they do anything in particular. They did not pretend to be in a car or airplane, in a house or on a boat… They were just entranced by the experience of sitting in a box.

BOX AS HOME
not playing

Sometimes occupying a box is a more serious matter.

Houses are sometimes disparagingly referred to as 'boxes'. But for some people a box might be their house.

The cardboard from which boxes are made can have advantageous properties. They provide insulation against the cold of a concrete pavement. Their sides can shield an occupant from drafts. They can contain belongings.

But most of all they identify a place. The assemblage of boxes illustrated above provide the centre, the point of reference for the homeless man who lives in them. They hold his belongings in place and, like the girl's loop on page 125, both stop those belongings from going astray and protect them from thieves.

A homeless person has constructed a sophisticated home for himself from cardboard boxes. He is sheltered by the roof of an underpass. But he shields himself from drafts with walls, which also contain his bedding and his belongings.

'Dans Paris il y a une rue;
Dans cette rue il y a une maison;
Dans cette maison il y a un escalier;
Dans cet escalier il y a une chambre;
Dans cette chambre il y a une table;
Sur cette table il y a un tapis;
Sur ce tapis il y a une cage;
Dans cette cage il y a un nid;
Dans ce nid il y a un œuf;
Dans cet œuf il y a un oiseau.'

'In Paris there is a street;
In that street there is a house;
In that house there is a stair;
Off that stair there is a room;
In that room there is a table;
On that table there is a cloth;
On that cloth there is a cage;
In that cage there is a nest;
In that nest there is an egg;
In that egg there is a bird.'

Paul Eluard – '**Dans Paris**'/'In Paris', 1942.

'The actual world is less intense than the world of his invention.'

Tennessee Williams – 'The Catastrophe of Success', in *The New York Times*, 1947.

BUILDING PLACES

The homeless man on the opposite page has built his home from cardboard boxes. Many of the places we use and occupy as children are places that we recognise as such. To recognise and use a place is in itself to be an architect. But often we want to make changes, to add to a place, or even to make a new place: such as an encampment on an expansive, pristine, recently tide-washed beach; or a simple platform house high in the branches of a tree. To amend a place, or to create a completely new place, involves building. Building is the means by which the mental, imaginative processes of architecture are made real. By building we change the actual world not just the world in our imaginations. And by doing so we change the world that other people see and experience. As architects we can build for ourselves; we can also build for others.

BUILDING
a bivouac

Building a simple bivouac on the beach is an engaging activity. You must find enough suitable material and then arrange it into an unnatural form.

The emotion aroused by crawling inside such a lair is different. The achievement of building is to create a place of refuge – of shade or shelter – a womb separated from the rest of the world, made especially stark by its juxtaposition with open land and sea stretching as far as the horizon.

All your senses are stimulated by crawling inside such a place. It is darker to the eyes. Sound is different. It is probably not as dry in rain as you might like. You feel the sand and pebbles with your hands, knees and backside. You smell the desiccated salty wood and seaweed, and even taste it at the back of your mouth. Building is about a lot more than construction.

There is fun in the construction of a bivouac, arranging material – in this case driftwood – into an unnatural formation by the application of strength, dexterity and ingenuity. The result can elicit an emotion of pride in the achievement. But entering the built place, as a place for inhabitation, can elicit other emotions.

BUILDING A PLACE IN THE SHIFTING SEA
rising above the waves

If there is a zone where you might think it is impossible to identify a place, it would probably be the surface of the ever-shifting sea. But when a student (above) was asked to make a place on the beach she set about defying this apparent impossibility. From driftwood and lengths of boat-abandoned rope she set about constructing a platform for herself in the rising tide. On this she sat surrounded by ocean, a fixed point amidst eternal movement.

Maybe for security, maybe not to occupy valuable land, for many centuries people across the world have been building their houses on stilts in rivers or lakes (right). A contemporary equivalent would be an oil rig platform, built to provide a stable base for drilling into the earth...; or perhaps a luxurious hotel in the Indian Ocean.

This roughly-assembled 'throne' sits as fixed place in the ever-moving waters of the ocean.

People around the world have been building lake dwellings on stilts for thousands of years.

MY TREE HOUSE 1
built with my friend when we were about 10

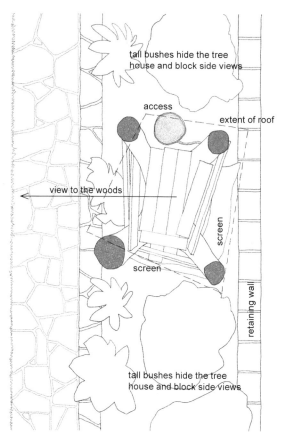

tall bushes hide the tree house and block side views

access

extent of roof

view to the woods

screen

screen

retaining wall

tall bushes hide the tree house and block side views

The tree house occupied a pre-recognised place, accessible by an easy climb and cupped by four branches fanning from a main trunk. Access was by a step – a stump – and a rope.

The first task was to build a flat floor on which one could stand securely. Seats and protective rails were added, and a fabric roof and walls to screen the interior from the house and the school yard.

Though hidden by trees and its in-built screen walls, the interior had views across the lawn to the woods beyond in one direction, and through 'loop-holes' (gaps in the screen) down into the school yard and across to the hills in the other (opposite). Each of its six directions was modulated by its architecture: floor and canopy; flanking trees; screens and open view.

Though built clumsily, our tree house did display some characteristics born of a common intuitive human capacity for architecture. I remember that the making of the tree house was more engaging than the occupation of it. I enjoyed cutting, fitting and fixing the planks, hammering nails into the trunks. I remember the thrill of making a new place that had not existed before; a place that had emerged from my mind and action; a place belonging to me. I did sit in it, though mainly to consider what I could add. It was arranged so I was hidden from the main house. I remember too the prospects: across the lawn of our garden to the woods on the slope opposite; down into the neighbouring school yard, and further to the hills beyond.

Looking back I can see architectural characteristics of the tree house that I could not have crystallised in words at the time. The tree house was a refuge with prospects. It was transcendent, lifting me and my friend above the ordinary world. It provided a centre – related to each of the six directions – and a datum, a reference point that belonged to us and no-one else. It occupied a liminal position: in-between the private garden and the open world outside. It provided a frame for the imagination: the self-image of independence and self-determination, but also narratives of defence against attack and journeying to distant places.

Whether acknowledged or not, all these characteristics have potential in 'grown-up' architecture too.

MY TREE HOUSE 2
a point of view

The tree was chosen because its four fanning branches already defined a place into which one could climb.

The tree stood in a border on the upper side of a retaining wall built to level ground for a school play yard next door. The tree house commanded various prospects.

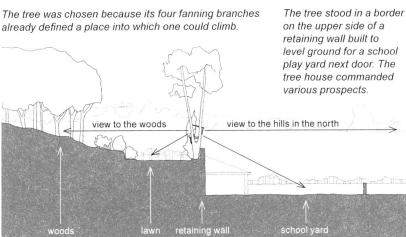

view to the woods

view to the hills in the north

woods   lawn   retaining wall   school yard

GILL'S SCHOOL YARD ARCHITECTURE
extending caves (at the age of five or six)

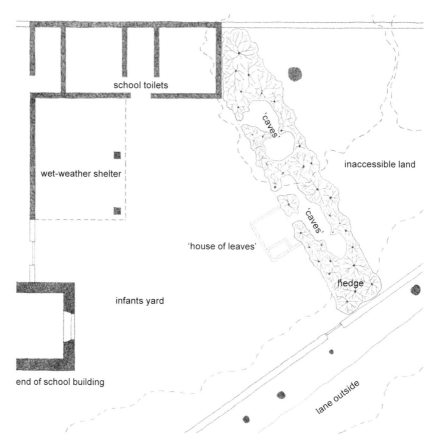

school toilets

'caves'

inaccessible land

wet-weather shelter

'caves'

'house of leaves'

hedge

infants yard

end of school building

lane outside

Nobody remembers everything about what they did when they were five or six years old, but my wife Gill remembers making dens in her primary school yard.

The youngest children – the infants – had their own play yard at the back of the school (above). It was bounded by: the end of the school building (which had been converted from a church); a wall between it and the yard for the older children, against which was a wet-weather shelter; a tree-shaded wall along a lane outside; and a thick hedge.

Though the yard provided the setting, the thick hedge was the site of Gill's recollection. Within it were 'caves' of space between the branches, which were the children's favourite places to hide. Sometimes they would break off branches as brushes to sweep dust and leaves into neat walls as an extension to the caves. Where the caves were irregular, the extensions picked up on the regular orthogonal geometry of the buildings the children were used to inhabiting.

Gill and her school friends drew imaginary houses on the school yard as extensions to the caves inside the hedge. They outlined walls with leaves brushed into neat straight lines. Sometimes they were subdivided with interior walls making bedrooms.

These extensions picked up the rectangular geometry of orthodox architecture. They also modified the transition between outside and inside the 'caves'.

MEDIATING BETWEEN SANCTUARY AND WORLD
the apron of a cave

Gill and her friends' school yard architecture (opposite) displays an intuitive grasp of a spatial pattern evident in more permanent architecture through history; an apt example of the innate architect at work.

In prehistoric times, on clement days, it is more likely that we would have conducted our daily lives around the opening of our cave rather than in its dark dank interior. Even so, we would have valued the possibility of retreat into the refuge that the cave offered. We were like molluscs able to withdraw into a protective shell.

Nowadays we could do the same thing when we go to a beach. We might 'take possession' of a cave but make our camp on its apron (top right).

In some traditional architectures around the world, such as these farm houses near the ancient city of Nalut in Libya (right), the irregular spaces of natural caves (like those in Gill's school hedge) are extended outwards into the world with walls that follow the geometry of making so they can easily support simple roofs. The coolness of the cave interior contrasts with the bright heat of the outdoors. A transitional hierarchy is created from the open and public world through the courtyard to the private concealed refuges of the caves within the natural living rock.

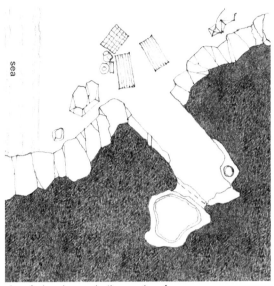

sea

plan of a beach camp by the opening of a cave

section

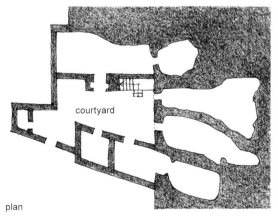

courtyard

plan

ROBINSON CRUSOE'S FIRST HOUSE

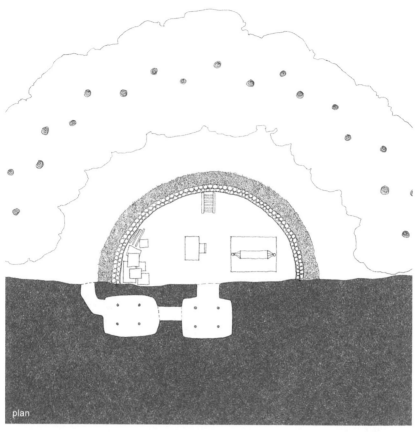

plan

In *The Life and Strange Surprizing Adventures of Robinson Crusoe, Of York, Mariner: Who lived Eight and Twenty Years, all alone in an un-inhabited Island on the Coast of America, near the Mouth of the Great River of Oroonoque; Having been cast on Shore by Shipwreck, wherein all the Men perished but himself* (1719), Daniel Defoe describes Crusoe as having constructed for himself two houses. The developed form of the first house is illustrated above. Its construction went through various stages (described opposite). These are presented in some detail in the novel. Its underlying architectural form – its idea of spatial organisation – is similar to the examples of place-making described on the previous two pages, especially Gill's hedge caves and house.

Robinson Crusoe built a house under a cliff. First he defined a semicircular area, which he eventually defended with a wall. From this he excavated caves into the rock of the cliff. (Compare with the 'fortress' on page 134.)

Crusoe's dwelling is an example of how we relate to the opportunities and challenges of the land in which we find ourselves. He acts and reacts with the directness of a child.

ROBINSON CRUSOE'S DESCRIPTION
of his place-making on the island

'Oct. 26. I walked about the shore almost all day to find out a place to fix my habitation, greatly concerned to secure myself from an attack in the night, either from wild beasts or men. Towards night I fixed upon a proper place under a rock, and marked out a semicircle for my encampment, which I resolved to strengthen with a work, wall, or fortification made of double stakes, lined within with cables, and without with turf...

'Nov. 1. I set up my tent under a rock, and lay there for the first night, making it as large as I could with stakes driven in to swing my hammock upon.

'Nov. 2. I set up all my chests and boards, and the pieces of timber which made my rafts, and with them formed a fence round me, a little within the place I had marked out for my fortification...

'Nov. 17. This day I began to dig behind my tent into the rock, to make room for my farther conveniency. Note, Three things I wanted exceedingly for this work, viz. a pickaxe, a shovel, and a wheel-barrow or basket; so I desisted from my work, and began to consider how to supply that want, and make me some tools...

'Nov. 23. My other work having now stood still, because of my making these tools, when they were finished I went on, and working every day, as my strength and time allowed, I spent eighteen days entirely in widening and deepening my cave, that it might hold my goods commodiously...

'Dec. 10. I began now to think my cave or vault finished, when on a sudden (it seems I had made it too large) a great quantity of earth fell down from the top and one side, so much that in short it frighted me, and not without reason too; for if I had been under it I had never wanted a gravedigger. Upon this disaster I had a great deal of work to do over again; for I had the loose earth to carry out, and, which was of more importance, I had the ceiling to prop up, so that I might be sure no more would come down...

'Dec. 17. From this day to the twentieth I placed shelves, and knocked up nails on the posts to hang every thing up that could be hung up: and now I began to be in some order within doors.

'Dec. 20. Now I carried every thing into the cave, and began to furnish my house, and set up some pieces of boards like a dresser, to order my victuals upon; but boards began to be very scarce with me: also I made me another table...

'Jan. 3. I began my fence or wall; which, being still jealous of my being attacked by somebody, I resolved to make very thick and strong...

'When this wall was finished, and the outside double fenced with a turf wall raised up close to it, I persuaded myself that if any people were to come on shore there, they would not perceive any thing like a habitation; and it was very well I did so, as may be observed hereafter...

'I worked excessive hard these three or four months to get my wall done; and the 14th of April I closed it up, contriving to go into it, not by a door, but over the wall by a ladder, that there might be no sign in the outside of my habitation.

'April 16. I finished the ladder; so I went up with the ladder to the top, and then pulled it up after me, and let it down on the inside: this was a complete enclosure to me; for within I had room enough, and nothing could come at me from without, unless it could first mount my wall. The very next day after this wall was finished, I had almost had all my labour overthrown at once, and myself killed; the case was thus: As I was busy in the inside of it behind my tent, just in the entrance into my cave, I was terribly frighted with a most dreadful surprising thing indeed; for on a sudden I found the earth come crumbling down from the roof of my cave, and from the edge of the hill, over my head, and two of the posts I had set up in the cave cracked in a frightful manner: I was heartily scared, but thought nothing of what was really the cause, only thinking that the top of my cave was falling in, as some of it had done before; and for fear I should be buried in it, I ran forward to my ladder, and not thinking myself safe there neither, I got over my wall for fear of the pieces of the hill which I expected might roll down upon me. I was no sooner stept down upon the firm ground, but I plainly saw it was a terrible earthquake...

'I worked daily two or three hours at enlarging my cave; and, by degrees, worked it on towards one side, till I came to the outside of the hill, and made a door or way out, which came beyond my fence or wall; and so I came in and out this way: but I was not perfectly easy at lying so open; for as I had managed myself before, I was in a perfect enclosure, whereas now I thought I lay exposed; and yet I could not perceive that there was any living thing to fear, the biggest creature that I had seen upon the island being a goat.'

CAVE AND FORECOURT
natural cave: artificial cave

In the beach camp above the tent is an artificial cave with a forecourt at its mouth defined by mats and windbreaks, and roofed with parasols.

The nave of a typical church (below) can be analysed as an enclosed 'forecourt' on the apron of the 'cave' of the sanctuary.

One could cite numerous further examples, of many different kinds...

This architectural strategy, realised in constructed buildings, seems to have originated in our prehistoric relationship with caves. That relationship is not, perhaps, a matter of precedent and influence (i.e. doing what has been done before) but more an example of the innate architect at work. People in different places at different times see the power in this architectural strategy.

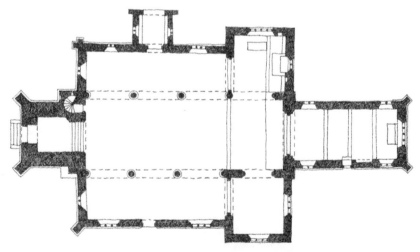

St Swithin's Church, Compton Bassett, England

GRASS VERGE
a special zone

'(Grass verges) are easily the most exciting and beautiful thing in this street! You are magic to any child raised on 20th-century estates, for you – wide, communal strip of grass between the pavement and the black-tar road – you are our place. You are miniature suburban village greens.'

Caitlin Moran – 'Why I Love Grass Verges', *The Times Magazine*, 10 June 2017.

We have grass verges outside our house. I play tennis and cricket there with my granddaughter. They have been used in various other ways too, by other children in the road.

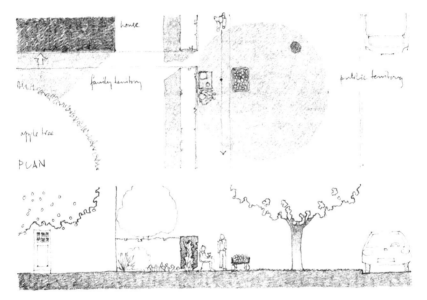

As reported in *Exercises in Architecture: Learning to Think as an Architect* (2012, page 4), when our neighbours had a particularly good crop of apples, their daughter would turn the grass verge into a shop (above). Sitting under the shade of a tree, she would put a barrow of apples on the grass and a table alongside her (for bags and the money). This installation became a place of transaction, the beginnings of a shop.

Other children have sometimes found the grass verge a good place to lay a rug for a picnic on a sunny day (below left).

section

In Matsetsa (Russia; right) I saw a lady who had set up a stall to sell blackberries to tourists (right). Not allowed in the grounds, she had to do so through the railings.

plan

KIT OF PARTS 1
on the beach

On the beach we employ a limited kit of ready-made parts to create our encampments. We use them in a wide variety of ways. The basic kit includes:

- towels, rugs and beach mats – to define an area of ground and to change its nature;
- folding or deck chairs – to sit on, but also to define space;
- windbreaks – to shelter from breeze, but also to screen and to define space;
- parasols – to shade or shelter, but also to act as markers;
- tents – to create refuge (e.g. for changing) but also to define space;
- ...

With this limited 'vocabulary of elements' we are able to 'write' a seemingly infinite variety of 'sentences'. In the language of architecture the kit of parts available to us on the beach enables us to produce a seemingly infinite variety of encampment compositions. As in verbal language, our spatial compositions seem to follow syntactic rules (see also page 90).

ANALYSING ARCHITECTURE NOTEBOOKS

KIT OF PARTS 2
in the house

*The artist Fabrice Gygi
has played on the idea of
the places we make under
tables in his 'Table Tent'
(1993; right).*

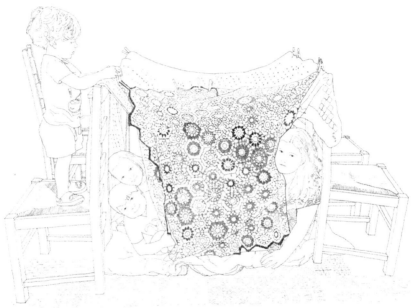

*A den conjured from
furniture and blankets
is fun to construct and
intriguing to inhabit: a
place to hide...*

As children we tend to use a kit of available parts
to indulge our innate capacity for architecture
(above) in and around the home. We rearrange
chairs and tables, requisition blankets and duvets,
pinch clothes pegs... and use them for our
constructions. We make dens, houses, caves,
trains, ships that sail the distant seas... But the
primary magic lies in creating a hidden interior
separated from everywhere else. There we can be
alone, or in an architecturally defined group with
our friends.

*'Diamond... was busy making a cave by the side of
his mother's fire, with a broken chair, a three-legged
stool, and a blanket, and then sitting in it.'*

George MacDonald – *At the Back of the North Wind* (1871),
2001; drawing (left) by Arthur Hughes.

AD HOC MOSQUE
a special place created with rugs and a chair

A mosque in the desert (below left) need be no more than a defined area of ground indicating the direction of Mecca. The Israelites' Tabernacle (below right) was made from a kit of parts too.

In 1999, in Nazareth, permission was granted for a large new mosque. Before construction began (and during some controversy) the site, a car park, was occupied by an ad hoc temporary mosque. It was created with a kit of parts that included carpets, kerbstones, and pipes; the direction of Mecca was indicated by a chair. On hot days it was shaded with cloth. Permission for the new mosque was revoked in 2002.

164

'From the window of my room in the University I used to be able to see beyond the high back-garden wall a typical small builder's yard. It was stacked with ladders of all lengths, planks, barrels, packing cases, house bricks, sacks of cement and plaster, wheelbarrows, buckets, spades, saws, tools of many fascinating shapes and varieties… The whole place, were it not for the high protecting wall and the double-barred gate, was a children's dream of heaven! There were hundreds of dark and dusty places to explore; there were innumerable possibilities in the way of quickly erected hidey-holes; those pieces of timber would make a stockade for Long John Silver; that little platform was simply crying out for a Superman take-off. Any child with any imagination and any fund of "comic" lore in his memory could improvise endless happy hours in such a place.'

John Barron Mays – *Adventure in Play*, 1957.

PLACES OF THE IMAGINATION

We do not always live in the actual world around us. We like to be transported to others in our imaginations. Perhaps we do this more than we might think. When we read a book or newspaper our thoughts are transported to other places. When we watch television or a film almost all our attention can be absorbed by their depictions of somewhere else. Even when we communicate with our friends and family, using phones or social media, our consciousness occupies some in-between shared zone. The world we actually occupy, including via those various media, is more multi-layered and complex than perhaps we think. But the actual, real places we make as children – as architects – provide other worlds for us too.

OTHER WORLDS
transporting our minds somewhere else

Sometimes it seems that we would prefer to live in our imaginations rather than in the real world. People on buses or trains prefer to be in the other world of their smart phones rather than with their fellow passengers.

As children we engage in play, and play often involves being somewhere else, creating a somewhere else to be.

When, as children, we discover books, we are fascinated by their content, the pictures and then the words that introduce us to concepts and ideas, places and stories that are provoked in our imaginations.

In this, as in other things, we remain children all our lives, fascinated by the capacity for our imaginations to be transported to other places, by words, pictures, sounds… and by architecture.

A small boy sits on a stair looking at a book. In doing so he has identified that stair as a place for reading. But the place he is occupying is a different one. It is the place to which the content of the book – its words and pictures – is taking him… in his imagination.

When I am draw/writing these Notebooks, as when designing buildings or tutoring students, I am in another world – a world of imagination.

SANDCASTLE
constructing pretend worlds

We can live nowhere else other than in our imaginations. That there is a boundary between reality and imagination is a myth born of our imaginations. We imagine there is reality. We project imagination onto it. Architecture deals, at its root, in imagination. Imagination is evident in the places we make on the beach. Sometimes, if we want to build a castle or a city, it can, for practical reasons, only be in model form – a sandcastle. When we have the resources, the power, the wealth, the will… we do it full scale, 'in reality'. But where is the difference, except in scale?

We see and experience a building as real, but it provides us with, frames us in, a world dreamt up in the imagination of its architect. When there, or even when not, we inhabit his or her imagination.

Playing with these sandcastles (right), you can imagine climbing steps and ramps, shooting arrows from the tops of towers, marching along winding pathways, attacking portals, defending battlements…

Some sandcastles are no more than shaped mounds of damp sand, but more elaborate examples (above and below) can become worlds in themselves, into which you can project your imagination. You can see in your mind's eye, and impersonate with your walking fingers, people inhabiting their spaces, defending their battlements, attacking their entrances. Here in miniature is the architectural imagination's capacity to conjure up worlds.

TABLE TOP AS ARENA
a distinct realm of the imagination

In an Istanbul café, where his parents work all the hours that are made, a small boy creates a world on a table top. It is his main playground.

The simple rectangle, separated from the ordinary world around, becomes, in his imagination, a motorway, a race track, a car park, the scene of crashes and devastating fires that have to be extinguished, a corniche where a Ferrari or Porsche owner can cruise flamboyantly or speed recklessly...

The table top is also, of course, a place – an altar, a plinth, an arena... physically separate from the real world – on which to display proudly a collection of toy cars, across which to spin diverting narratives, into which to disappear from the everyday world into a fantasy land of the imagination.

A table top is a special zone, an arena for a meal. Here a child has adopted that special zone as a place to play with his collection of toy vehicles.

What else is the Acropolis in Athens other than the Athenians displaying their collection of temples on the 'table top' of the craggy rock standing in the centre of their city; establishing a realm for the narratives of gods?

TEA PARTY
pretence and reality

A child plays tea party at a cloth laid on the floor by her mother. Even though young she recognises the meaning of the place and acts accordingly. Her guests are her toys. She acts with assiduous hospitality offering them tea, in cups or directly from the tea pot.

Whereas some places for imaginative play are conceptually a long way from their real counterparts – a table top (opposite), for example, is very different from a motorway, race track, or car park – a pretend tea party is very close in form to its 'real' counterpart. One might say the only difference is the absence of (the risk of) hot liquids: the cups may be smaller, but the above drawing could be a depiction of a real tea party.

But perhaps what we call a 'real' tea party is just as much a game, a matter of pretence...

Children learn about adult behaviour through imaginative play. Here a small girl entertains her toys to tea, enjoying the role of host. In this case the focal arena – the architecture of the occasion – is not a table top but a cloth laid on the floor. Though the cloth was laid by her mother, the child clearly understands and engages with the meaning of the place and will learn to be the architect of such places in the future.

DOLLS HOUSE
projecting our imaginations…

There is no clear conceptual line dividing places of the imagination and those that we inhabit in our daily lives. All the places we inhabit, even those in the wilderness, are products of our own imaginations. The cities and houses, offices and schools, we live and work in… are that too. But they are the products of the imaginations of their architects as well.

 The places we make as children are creatures of our imaginations. We make them along a conceptual continuum, from those miniature models (sandcastles for example) that can clearly not be inhabited; through dolls houses and puppet theatres which can accommodate pretend people and their lives; to 'pretend' shops which are, architecturally speaking, just as real as their 'real' counterparts (see page 161).

We can project our imaginations into the miniature world of a dolls house… projecting life into its architecture.

'I imagine a Parisian apartment building whose façade has been removed… so that all the rooms in the front, from the ground floor to the attics, are instantly and simultaneously visible.'
Georges Perec, trans. Sturrock – 'Species of Spaces' (1974), 1997.

PUPPET THEATRE
... to manipulate dolls or puppets (or people?)

We can manipulate the characters in a puppet theatre (above)...

... or those (our avatars) on the infinite battlefield of a computer game.

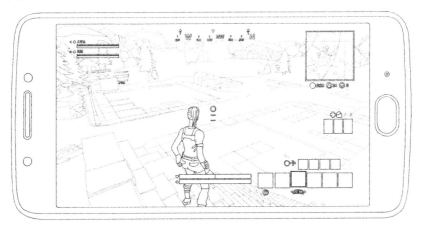

IMAGINING THE WORLD
all architecture's a stage, an imagined frame for life

But then all architecture conjures an imagined world. A child's journey into architecture is into imagining worlds for others to inhabit, as well as themselves.

Scamozzi's imagined city in Palladio's Teatro Olimpico, Vicenza, (1585).

ENDNOTE

As children we are not interested in architectural style or ornamentation; we are not interested in straight lines, perfect squares and circles nor subtle geometric proportions; we are not interested in producing mesmerising drawings nor complicated computer-aided constructions; and we cannot be, because of the technical challenges, particularly interested in weatherproofing or structural sophistication. We may not, as children, be interested in all those things that have preoccupied professional architects through history; but we are interested in place-making. We are interested in situating ourselves in the world. To situate yourself in the world is an a priori corollary of being alive. To make a place for yourself is to project your imagination onto the world around you, changing it according to your ideas, needs and desires. To do this lies at the heart of being an architect.

We gradually become aware of ourselves in this strange world. For some time when we are very young we have to be content with being put in our place. Our parents help us, look after us, by putting us in safe places: our mother's arms; a cot; a play mat; a high chair; a buggy... But gradually we become able to put ourselves in places. Step by step, we begin exploring, wandering, and, subject to (or despite) parental authority, choose which places to put ourselves. We begin to become aware of when and how we are doing that and of when we are settled in a specific place. Specific places are like security blankets; when we are in them we know where we are. That is a sentiment that never leaves us. Wandering is interesting; being settled in a place is security. Even in our early lives we want a combination of both.

Initially we settle in places that we recognise as such: our father's lap; at our mother's side; on a cushion; under a table. But gradually we realise that we are agents of change; we can alter the world. By exercising our powers of recognition and choice we have awoken our architectural instinct. But we then take it further and begin to make places for ourselves. We make a nest of cushions or hang a blanket as a curtain across one side of a table; we collect discarded cardboard boxes and sit inside them, or build them into a house. We can intervene, rearrange things so that we make places of our own. Through these steps we rely on the innate architect within. We learn things as we go but our capacity for architecture, our architectural faculty, is hard-wired in our brains.

For a few years we are free to enjoy and develop this capacity. Even in preschool playgroups and nursery we might continue to build dens and arrange our friends in formal groups for games and dances. Gradually 'more important' challenges begin to usurp our architectural instincts. In formal education, development of language and mathematics takes priority. Our innate architect languishes in unemployment, only resurfacing occasionally when we go on scout camps, spend a day by the sea or want to light a fire in the woods.

As we grow up, just about all the places we occupy and use are places that are made for us. The schools, the houses, the shops, the doctors surgeries... are all provided, designed by others. We have no say in how they are. There are good reasons for this. The physical world in which we live, our built environment, would be chaotic if anarchy prevailed and every one of us was free to make significant and permanent places for ourselves.

Sophisticated buildings and shared places require substantial funding and coordinated design. But someone has to design those sophisticated shared buildings and places. Poets, playwrights, novelists, politicians, songwriters, lawyers... all use language professionally. They have the advantage that language has been one of the two main focuses of education throughout their schooling. Mathematicians, scientists, surveyors, engineers... all use mathematics professionally. They too have the advantage that mathematics has enjoyed detailed coverage in their education.

But what of architects? What of those people who have to design those places – schools, houses, shops... – professionally, for others to use. Language and mathematics are useful but neither is key. The core faculty for architecture – which we demonstrated when we were young but has been left to become dormant – is the ability to conjure places out of our surroundings. Its rudimentary potential is evident in the examples illustrated in this Notebook.

Place is the seed and core of all architecture. Place is the equivalent in architecture of the meaning that lies in words. Identification of place is the first proposition of every work of architecture ever produced. And all these things are evident in the places we make as children. What we are seeing in the places we make as children – whatever age we might be and in whatever circumstances we find ourselves – is nothing less than the innate language of architecture by which we make sense, spatially, of the world around us.

What we as children are doing when we make places is a mode of creative research. This kind of research is not the same as that which we call scientific, which conducts experiments to understand how natural phenomena work. The research in place-making is into our own relationship with and agency in the world: it explores what we can do to alter the world to accommodate our selves, our possessions, our activities, our gods…

And so, the fundamental message of this Notebook is to remember that, if you want to become an architect, you are one already. You have been an architect – an architect of your world – since you emerged from the womb. Even if you do want to become preoccupied with those concerns mentioned at the beginning of this Endword, remember that place-making comes first.

'Most adults can remember what it was like to play as a child. For the majority, the most enjoyable times of play were not in the designated areas designed by adults, but instead through occupying the streets, the back garden and any other part of the environment that was accessible to them. It is during this period that children learn about the world around them, learn valuable social skills and perhaps most importantly, learn about themselves. This incidental play is paramount to a child's development, and children inherently have an ability to find opportunities for this play anywhere.'

Emma Kitley – *Playing for Citizenship: Reinstating the Urban Child*, 2016.

ACKNOWLEDGEMENTS

I must thank Gillian Clarke, National Poet of Wales 2008–16, for her kind permission to use some lines from her poem 'Letting the Light In'.

I would also like to thank: Adrian Bailey, Zoë Berman (who was the tutor for some of the student projects illustrated), Alice Brownfield, Seth Burke, Reggie Burke, Mary Crawley, Jack Crawley, Emily Dawson, Fran Ford, Merve Kaptan Unwin, Emma Kitley, Maria Kylin, Christina O'Brien, Alan Paddison, William Quaile, Emily Stanley, David Unwin, Eugenia Baibazarova Unwin, Idris Unwin, Jim Unwin, Nina Unwin, Trudy Varcianna, Mary Wrenn.

All my writing on architecture has, to some extent, been autobiographical. It has drawn extensively on my travels and attempts to find ways to teach architecture. It has benefited from insights prompted by interactions with students and colleagues. But in some ways the content of this particular Notebook is the most personal. The vast majority of the examples and illustrations are drawn from my observations of my own children and grandchildren as they have grown. And so it is to them, as well as to the anonymous architects of other examples included in this Notebook, that I offer my greatest thanks.

I want also to thank Gill for her continued good-humoured encouragement; and for spotting the 'I♡u' with a hand print (see page 47) on the dirty window of a Cardiff bus.

BIBLIOGRAPHY

Kathryn Aalto – *The Natural World of Winnie-the-Pooh*, Timber Press, Portland, Oregon, 2015.

Jay Appleton – *The Experience of Landscape*, Wiley, London, 1975.

Aristotle, trans. Hardie and Gaye – *Physics* (350 BCE), Oxford U.P., 1930.

Gaston Bachelard, trans. Jolas – *Poetics of Space* (1958), Beacon Press, Boston, 1964.

R. Scott Bakker – *The Thousandfold Thought: The Prince of Nothing, Book 3*, Hachette, London, 2006.

Walter Benjamin, trans. Jephcott and Shorter – 'Naples' (1924) and 'One-Way Street' (1925–6), in *One-Way Street and Other Writings*, Verso, London, 1985.

Alan Bennett – *The Madness of George III*, Faber & Faber, London, 1992.

Michèle Bernstein, trans. Kelsey – *All the King's Horses* (1960), MIT Press, 2008.

Donna Birdwell-Pheasant – 'The Home "Place": Center and Periphery in Irish House and Family Systems', in Birdwell-Pheasant and Lawrence Zúñiga, eds. – *House Life: Space, Place and Family in Europe*, Berg, London, 1999.

William Blake – *The Marriage of Heaven and Hell* (1793), in Keynes, ed. – *Blake: Complete Writings*, Oxford U.P., 1976.

Enid Blyton – *Hollow Tree House*, Arrow Books, London, 1987.

O.F. Bollnow, trans. Christine Shuttleworth, Joseph Kohlmaier, ed. – *Human Space* (1963), Hyphen Press, London, 2011.

Anthony Buckeridge – *Jennings' Little Hut* (1951), Stratus Books, Kelly Bray, Cornwall, 2001.

Catherine Burke – 'Fleeting Pockets of Anarchy: Streetwork. The Exploding School', in *Pedagogica Historica*, 11 June 2014.

Roger Callois, trans. Meyer Barash – *Man, Play and Games* (1961), University of Illinois Press, 2001.

Tony Chilton – *Fair Play for Children: Adventure Playgrounds, a Brief History*, (1973), 2013; available at: fairplayforchildren.org/pdf/1397922953.pdf (November 2018).

Gillian Clarke – 'Letting the Light In', in *Recipe for Water*, Carcanet Press, Manchester, 2009.

Richard Dattner – *Design for Play*, Van Nostrand Reinhold, 1969.

Emily Dawson and William Quaile – *Landscape*, Welsh School of Architecture, Cardiff, 2016.

Daniel Defoe – *The Life and Strange Surprizing Adventures of Robinson Crusoe, Of York, Mariner: Who lived Eight and Twenty Years, all alone in an un-inhabited Island on the Coast of America, near the Mouth of the Great River of Oroonoque; Having been cast on Shore by Shipwreck, wherein all the Men perished but himself* (1719); available at: gutenberg.org/ebooks/521 (January 2019)

Gilles Deleuze and Félix Guattari, trans. Massumi – '1837: Of the Refrain', in *A Thousand Plateaus* (1987), Continuum, London, 2004.

Dionysius of Halicarnassus, trans. Cary – *Roman Antiquities* (1st C. BCE), Harvard U.P., 1937; available at: penelope.uchicago.edu/Thayer/E/Roman/Texts/Dionysius_of_Halicarnassus/ home.html (November 2018).

Émile Durkheim, trans. Joseph Ward Swain – *The Elementary Forms of the Religious Life* (1912), Oxford U.P., 2008.

Mircea Eliade, trans. Sheed – *Patterns in Comparative Religion*, Sheed and Ward, London, 1958.

Mircea Eliade, trans. Trask – *The Sacred and the Profane: the Nature of Religion*, Harcourt Brace, San Diego, 1957.

T.S. Eliot – 'The Waste Land' (1922);
    available at: poetryfoundation.org/poems/47311/the-waste-land (January 2019).
Paul Eluard - 'Dans Paris' (1942); available at:
    lakanal.net/poesie/dansparis.htm (January 2019).
Per Olaf Fjeld – *Sverre Fehn: The Pattern of Thoughts*, Monacelli Press, New York, 2009.
Anne Frank – *The Diary of a Young Girl* (1947), Lifebooks, 2018.
Josie Gleave and Issy Cole-Hamilton – *A World Without Play*, Play England, Bristol, 2012.
Peter Gray – *Free to Learn*, Basic Books, New York, 2013.
Peter Gray – 'When Play is Learning', in *Phi Delta Kappa International*, Vol. 65, No. 9, May 1984.
Vittorio Gregotti – 'Address to the Architectural League, New York, 1982', in *Section A*, Vol. 1,
    No. 1, February/March 1983, p. 8.
Zane Grey – *Tales of Fishing Virgin Seas* (1925), Derrydale Press, Maryland, 2000.
Stephen Grosz – *The Examined Life: How We Lose and Find Ourselves*, Chatto & Windus, London,
    2013
Roger Hart – *Children's Experience of Place*, Irvington Publishers, New York, 1979.
Roger Hart – *Children's Participation: from Tokenism to Citizenship*, UNICEF International Child
    Development Centre, 1992.
Roger Hart – 'Children's Participation in Planning and Design', in Weinstein and David, eds., 1987,
    pp. 217–39.
Martin Heidegger, trans. Charles Seibert – 'Art and Space' (1973), in Neil Leach – *Rethinking
    Architecture*, Routledge, London, 1997, pp. 121–4.
Herman Hertzberger – *Space and Learning*, 010 Publishers, Rotterdam, 2007.
Homer, trans. Rieu – *The Iliad* (c. 700 BCE), Penguin, Harmondsworth, 1950.
Shirley Hughes – *Sally's Secret* (1973), Random House, London, 2002.
Johan Huizinga, trans. anon. – *Homo Ludens* (1944, 1950), Beacon Press, Boston, 1955.
Susan Isaacs – *Social Development in Young Children* (1933), Routledge, London, 1999.
Carl Gustav Jung, trans. Winston and Winston – *Memories, Dreams, Reflections* (1963), Collins,
    Glasgow, 1977.
Lia Karsten – *Children in the City*, Reclaim the Street, London, 2006.
Robert F. Kennedy – Speech at the University of Cape Town, South Africa, 6 June 1966;
    available at: rfksafilm.org/html/speeches/unicape.php (November 2018).
Harald Kimpel and Johanna Werckmeister – *Die Strandburg: Eine versandetes Freizeitvergnügen*,
    Jonas Verlag, Marburg, 1995.
Emma Kitley – *Playing for Citizenship: Reinstating the Urban Child*, unpublished dissertation,
    Bartlett School of Architecture, London, 2016.
Maria Kylin – 'Children's Dens', in *Youth and Environments*, Vol. 13, No. 1, Spring 2003.
Liane Lefaivre – *Ground-up City: Play as a Design Tool*, 010 Publishers, Rotterdam, 2007.
Primo Levi, trans. Rosenthal – *The Periodic Table*, Schocken, New York, 1975.
Adolf Loos, trans. Mitchell – 'Architecture' (1910), in Opel and Opel, eds. – *On Architecture:
    Writings by Adolf Loos*, Ariadne Press, Riverside, 2002.
Thomas Mann, trans. Lowe-Porter – *Joseph and His Brothers* (1933), Vintage, London, 1999.
Thomas Mann, trans. Lowe-Porter – *Joseph in Egypt* (1936), Vintage, London, 1999.
George MacDonald – *At the Back of the North Wind* (1871), Everyman, London, 2001.
Gabriel García Márquez, trans. Grossman – *Living to Tell the Tale*, Penguin, London, 2003.
Yann Martel – *Life of Pi* (2001), Knopf, London, 2003.
Graham Masterton – *Fire Spirit*, Severn House, Sutton, 2010.
John Barron Mays – *Adventure in Play*, Liverpool Council of Social Service, 1957.
Maurice Merleau-Ponty, Edie, ed., trans. Dallery – 'Eye and Mind' (1961), in *The Primacy of
    Perception* (1964), rev. by Smith in Johnson ed. – *The Merleau-Ponty Aesthetics Reader*,
    Northwest U.P., Evanston, 1993.
A.A. Milne – *When We Were Very Young*, Methuen, London, 1924.
Caitlin Moran – 'Why I Love Grass Verges', in *The Times Magazine*, 10 June 2017.
Charles P. Mountford – *Ayers Rock*, Angus & Robertson, Sydney, 1965.
John G. Neihardt – *Black Elk Speaks* (1932), University of Nebraska Press, 1979.
Catherine Nixey – 'Robert Harris: I'd be put off by the words "Booker winner" on the front', in *The
    Times* (Review Section), 16 September 2017.
Nils Norman – *An Architecture of Play: a Survey of London's Adventure Playgrounds*, Four Corners
    Books, London, 2003.
Juhani Pallasmaa – *The Eyes of the Skin*, Wiley, Chichester, 2005.
Georges Perec, trans. Sturrock – 'Species of Spaces' (1974), in *Species of Spaces and Other
    Essays*, Penguin, London, 1997.
Antoinette Portis – *Not a Box*, Harper Collins, New York, 2006.
Wolfgang Preiser, ed. – *Environmental Design Research: Volume One, Selected Papers*,
    Routledge, Abingdon, 2016.

Ellen Beate Hansen Sandseter – 'We Don't Allow Children to Climb Trees', in *American Journal of Play*, Vol. 8, No. 2, 2016.

Göran Schildt – *Alvar Aalto in his Own Words*, Rizzoli, New York, 1997.

Francesca Simon – *Horrid Henry's Stinkbomb*, Orion, London, 2002.

William Shakespeare – *As You Like It* (1623);
available at: shakespeare.mit.edu/asyoulikeit/full.html (January 2019).

Sarina Singh and others – *Aboriginal Australia & the Torres Strait Islands*, Lonely Planet, Melbourne, 2001.

Alison Smithson – 'Beatrix Potter's Places', in *Architectural Design*, Vol. 37, 1967.

Mayer Spivak – 'Archetypal Places', in *Architecture Forum*, 1973, pp. 44–50, reprinted in Preiser, ed., 2016, pp. 33–46.

John Steinbeck – *East of Eden* (1952), Penguin, London, 2000.

John Steinbeck – *Grapes of Wrath* (1939), Penguin, London, 2002.

John Steinbeck – *Tortilla Flat* (1935), Penguin, London, 1997.

Laurence Sterne – *Tristram Shandy* (1759), Oxford U.P., 1983.

Andrew Todd and Jean-Guy Lecat – *The Open Circle*, Palgrave Macmillan, New York, 2003.

Leo Tolstoy, trans. Louise and Aylmer Maude – *Anna Karenina* (1878), Penguin, Harmondsworth, 1995.

Simon Unwin – *Analysing Architecture* (1997), Routledge, Abingdon, 2014.

Simon Unwin – *Curve* (Analysing Architecture Notebook Series), Routledge, Abingdon, 2019.

Simon Unwin – *Exercises in Architecture*, Routledge, Abingdon, 2012.

Simon Unwin – *Metaphor* (Analysing Architecture Notebook Series), Routledge, Abingdon, 2019.

Simon Unwin – *The Ten Most Influential Buildings in History: Architecture's Archetypes*, Routledge, Abingdon, 2017.

Simon Unwin – *Twenty-Five Buildings Every Architect Should Understand*, Routledge, Abingdon, 2016.

Dom H. van der Laan, trans. Padovan – *Architectonic Space: Fifteen Lessons on the Disposition of the Human Habitat*, E.J. Brill, Leiden, 1983.

Fred Vargas, trans. Siân Reynolds – *The Chalk Circle Man* (1991), Vintage Books, London, 2009.

Colin Ward – *Child in the City*, Architectural Press, London, 1977.

Colin Ward – *Schools No Longer: Anarchy in Action*, George Allen and Unwin, London, 1973.

Carol Simon Weinstein and Thomas G. David, eds. – *Spaces for Children: the Built Environment and Child Development*, Plenum Press, New York, 1987.

Robert Westall – *The Machine Gunners*, Macmillan, London, 1975.

Tennessee Williams – 'The Catastrophe of Success', in *The New York Times*, 30 November 1947.

Tennessee Williams – *The Glass Menagerie* (1945), Penguin, London, 2009.

Penny Wilson – *The Playwork Primer*, Alliance for Childhood, New York, 2010.

INDEX

Aalto, Alvar 62
Acropolis, Athens 168
ad hoc shelter 57
agents of change 174
aggression 33
agoraphobia 41, 63, 109
allegiance 113
altar 39, 140
amniotic water 100
anarchy 174
another place 45
anthropomorphic toys 148
Appleton, Jay 50
apron of a cave 157, 160
architect of time 145
architectural instinct 174
architecture, a doing word 7
arena 94, 106, 112, 113, 137, 168
Aristotle 112
artificial cave 160
Astley, Neville 93
attention 132
audience 66, 139
avatar 171
axis mundi 140
Ayer's Rock (Uluru) 58, 78

bagpipes 82
Baker, Mark 93
Bakker, R. Scott 84
Baltic Sea sand fortresses 124
baptismal font 100
Barra 111
barricade 99
baseball 142
bastion against attack 124
battlefield 87, 137
beach 23, 24, 25, 34, 74, 75, 80, 102
bed sheet 79
Benjamin, Walter 42
Bennett, Alan 7
Berlin wall 85
Bernstein, Michèle 10
bivouac 152
blackboard 102
Black-E Arts Centre, Liverpool 55
Black Elk 134
Black Holes 49
Blake, William 3
blanket 89
book 166
Bouffes du Nord 139
boundary 66, 77, 95, 106, 107, 137, 142
box 147–50, 151
Brook, Peter 139
bubble 13, 130, 131, 138
building as natural setting 55
building places 151
burial 38
busking 82

cage 63
candle 79, 129
Casa Malaparte (Libera) 73
cat 31
catapult 37
cave 16, 17, 41, 46, 56, 156, 157, 163
celebration 129
centre 109, 122, 123, 141, 150, 154
centre of attention 132
ceremonial pathway 143
chair 33, 90
chalk line 135
challenge 71
chaos 115
chapter house 140
chess 87, 103
chora 5, 106, 112
church 37
circle 13, 85, 88, 109–46
circle as verb 128
circle of confinement 135
circle of conflict 137
circle of defence 134
circle of illumination 129
circle of movement 143
circle of performance 139
circle of protection 133
circle of shadow 59
circle of string 128
circle of unwanted attention 132
circle the wagons 134
circumcision 123
city wall 142
clarinettist 82
Clarke, Gillian viii
claustrophilia 147
clearing ground 20, 123
clockwise 143
closing eyes 40
clown 66
cock-fighting 138
collective cohesion 119
comfort 72
communal circle 141
computer-aided construction 173
computer game 171
conceptual twist 77
conflict 33, 87, 95
confrontation 103
connection 99
control 4, 103
Cooper, James 36
corpse 111
council chamber 140
court 105, 106
cradle 110, 118
cricket 106, 107
curtain 41, 42

dance 30, 67
dark 79
Dawson, Emily 36, 78
Defoe, Daniel 158
Deleuze, Gilles 115
den 3, 156, 163, 174
Dionysius of Halicarnassus 97
dispute 33
distortion 89
Dogville (von Trier) 102
dolls house 170
dominion 71
don't cross 97
door 42
doorway 25, 37
drawing 173
drawing a circle 113, 114
drawing attention 138
dreams 60
Dreamtime 78
driftwood 34
dune 37
dwelling 123
dwelling place 34

earth 52
earth house 48
Easter eggs 42
egg 111, 118
Eliot, T.S. 58
Eluard, Paul 151
emotion 28, 29, 80, 152
enigmatic power 122
envelopment 109, 110, 111, 114, 147
exclusion 116
expulsion 137

Fabian, Abbé K. 23
face-to-face 87, 105
falling off 77
family 126, 127
fantasy land 168
Fehn, Sverre 49, 53
'female' aspect of architecture 147
fire 34, 80, 123, 139, 141
fixing love 136
focal point 141
foetus 111
football 108
footsteps 75
fort 3, 119, 120, 121, 124, 127, 134
Fortress Caparetto 50
frame 30, 32, 33, 36, 37, 41, 62, 83, 106, 147,
    172
Frank, Anne 42
freedom 24
free entry 100
friends 35, 84, 98, 113, 163
furniture 99, 103

game 105, 106, 107, 108
gangs of Glenrothes 137
geometric proportions 173
geometry 83
German holiday-makers 124

Gilgal 121
goal 105
going round in circles 142
grass verge 161
grave 38
gravity 69
Gregotti, Vittorio 14
Grey, Zane 120
Grosz, Stephen viii
group formation 89
guard of honour 85
Guattari, Félix 115
Gwahoddiad 82
Gygi, Fabrice 163

hand outline, print, stencil 46–7
harbour 68
Harris, Robert 126
Hart, Roger A. viii, 3, 91
heart 123
hearth 123
Heidegger, Martin 123
hiding 41
hiding places 42
hokey cokey 83
hole digging 48
home 115
homeless people 58, 150
Homer 80, 87
Homo Ludens (Huizinga) 105
horizon 13, 35, 37, 49, 114
house 34, 150
huddle 85
Huizinga, Johan 105
human condition 4

I...
    I align 35
    I alter 20, 34
    I am 8, 114
    I am led 75
    I assemble 84
    I build 22
    I change the world 151
    I cherish 39
    I choose 32, 39
    I climb 70
    I commemorate 38
    I construct 22
    I contain 128, 150
    I cook 80
    I cross 11, 117
    I defend 33
    I define 91, 114
    I dig 22
    I display 39
    I draw a boundary 13
    I encircle 128
    I exhibit 39
    I fight 33
    I hide 19, 40, 43, 50
    I inhabit 17
    I jump 68
    I keep in place 125, 150
    I live 9

I make 22
I mark 14, 38
I modify 20
I occupy 17, 31, 130
I orient 35
I own 12, 95
I peep 44
I perform 138
I place 18
I point 15, 35
I possess 130, 157
I pretend 40
I project 71, 170
I protect 150
I put 18
I recognise 16, 30
I reflect 149
I see 16
I settle 72
I shout 82
I sign 21, 46
I sing 82
I spectate 138
I swing 69
I walk 10, 77
identification of place 2, 3, 5, 14, 19, 33, 67,
        104, 108, 116, 128, 129, 150, 153
Ik village 139
imagination 56, 148, 165–72
inclusion 116
individuation 45, 114, 122
inert body 9
inhabitation 54, 104
innate architect 1, 5, 90, 163, 174
innate geometry of body 83
insecurity 126
intuition 109
Isaacs, Susan 64
Istanbul 168

Jonas, Joan 111
Julius Caesar 27
Jung, C.G. 122

Kaptan, Merve 39
keep out 96
Kennedy, Robert F. 92
king of the castle 70
Kitley, Emma 175
kit of parts 162, 163

labyrinth 74
language, architecture as 1, 2, 3, 5, 6, 7, 27, 49,
        90, 109, 125, 127, 162, 175
Lerner, Alan Jay 41
Levi, Primo 135
Libbet, Neil 55
Libera, Adalberto 73
library 57
light 79
liminality 154
line 97, 126
line of movement 142
line of sight 15
lining up 4

linkage 15
loop of string 128
Loos, Adolf 38

MacDonald, George 163
Maeshowe, Orkney 146
magic 106
magical protection 125
magic circle 116, 117, 127
making sense 10, 11, 101, 175
mandala 122
Mann, Thomas 61, 109, 121
mantrap 125
marker 14, 38
Martel, Yann 94
Masai hunters 133
mass 52
Masterton, Graham 88
maternal refuge 147
matrix of routes 76
Matsetsa, Russia 161
Mays, John Barron 165
measuring time 144, 145, 146
Mecca 164
Merleau-Ponty, Maurice 115
metalanguage 83
metaphor 26, 27, 71, 75, 92, 114
metaphor of the cave 43
Milne, A.A. 65
modification 73
Moran, Caitlin 161
mosque 37, 164
Mountford, Charles P. 78
moving about 24
music 82
music festival 141

Nalut, Libya 157
narrative architecture 149, 168
narrative mapping 78, 79
national identity 38
natural abandon 67
natural environment as architecture 54
natural language of spatial relationship 1
naughty step 65
Nazareth 164
neighbour 33, 102
Neihardt, John G. 134
nest 174
newspaper 128
noise 82
nuclear bunker 48
numinous circle 122

Olds, Anita Rui 7
O'Neill, Ed 36
open circle 139
orientation 140
ornamentation 173
orthogonal geometry 156
outline 112, 113

Palladio, Andrea 172
Pallasmaa, Juhani 81
Parisian apartment building 170

parliament 140
Patel, Roshni 78
pathway 26, 27, 74–8, 141, 142, 143
paving stones 67
peeping 44
Peppa Pig (Astley and Baker) 93
Perec, Georges 170
perfect squares and circles 173
performance 66, 67
performance circle 138
perfume 37, 81
picnic 161
picturesque 36
pit 100
pitch 105, 106, 107, 108
place-making 1, 3, 20, 91, 109, 113, 114, 121,
    159, 173, 175
placing 39, 73
plan 13
platform in the sea 153
Plato 5, 43, 112
play 106
plough 97, 142
poetry 4
pointing 15, 36, 37
point of view 155
political, architecture as 33
polygon 88
Portis, Antoinette 147
possession 95
power 71
power of the circle 128
pram 118
prayer mat 94
presence 66, 71, 92, 114
pretence 169
pristine beach 116
privacy 19
procession 143
Proshansky, Harold M. 23
prospect 51, 155
protection 126
protective cocoon 118
protective loop 125
protective shell 157
protective shrine 136
prowess 77
psychological comfort 147
psychological security 110
psychology 41
psychotherapist 98, 103
puddle 93
puppet theatre 171
pyramid 38
pyre 80

Quaile, William 36, 78
quarantine 128

Reading Festival 141
receptacle of becoming 106, 112
recognition 73
refuge 29, 43, 44, 50, 51, 61, 119, 124, 152,
    157
remote 37

Riley, Sion 78
ring a ring a roses 83
ring of slime 130
ripples 92
ritual ground 123
Rivlin, Leanne 4
Robinson Crusoe (Defoe) 158, 159
rock 70, 71, 72
rock shelter 57, 58
Romulus 97, 142
room 96
rounders 142
route 142, 143
route finding 74
rudimentary architecture 4, 29, 113, 121
rudimentary place-making 7
rudimentary places 1
rudiments of architecture 3
rule system 26, 76

sacred 123
sacred realm of play 106
St Fagans National Museum of History 138
St Swithin's Church, Compton Bassett 160
sanctuary 157
sandcastle 167
Scamozzi 172
school 65
school yard architecture 156
sea 153
security 29, 173
sense 101
separation 45
shadow 60, 61, 121, 136, 144, 145
Shakespeare, William 66
Shaw, Leland G. 147
shop 161
shrine 128, 129, 136
side-by-side 86
signature 47
Simon, Francesca 81
sitting in the shade 57
six directions 154
Skara Brae 39
sleep 61
slime bubble 130
smart phone 166
smell 81, 152
social circle 52, 140, 141
social gathering 123
song 82, 115
songlines 78
sound 82
space 52
space, relationship with 5
spatial rules 101, 102, 162
special realm 129
sphere of illumination 79
sphere of influence 113
sphere of sound 82
spiral 127
spot 14
square 136
stage 30, 66, 67, 68, 94, 138, 172
stairs 65, 166

Steinbeck, John 63, 118, 147
Sterne, Laurence 109
stilt house 153
stinkbomb 81
stone 38
stone circle 122, 123, 146
story-telling 3, 147
straight lines 173
street football 108
string 78
study 104
style 173
summit 70, 71
sun clock 144
sundial 144, 145
sunset 121
swaddling 110
swing 69
syntax 90, 162

Tabernacle 164
table 42, 62, 64, 163, 174
table top 168
target 25
tea party 169
Teatro Olimpico, Vicenza (Palladio) 172
teeth 125
temple 37, 136
tennis player 136
tent 141
tents 90
terebinth 61
territory 33, 137
theatre 66
threshold 11, 27, 28, 29, 60, 95, 117, 138, 142
thrill 117
throwing out 137

tide 119, 120, 121
time 5, 144, 145, 146
togetherness 89
Tolstoy, Leo 79
tomb 111
top 70
tower of people 85
transition between outside and inside 156, 157
treasure 125
tree 16, 17, 21, 38, 59, 60, 61, 69
tree house 154, 155
Tristram Shandy (Sterne) 109
'Twigloo' 132
'Twilight' (Jonas) 111

Uluru (Ayer's Rock) 58, 78
umbrella 136
unity 126

van der Laan, Dom H. 52, 140
Vargas, Fred 129
verbs of architecture 7–22, 55
von Trier, Lars 102

wall 25, 77, 85, 95, 97
walls of leaves 156
warmth 80
watching the sun 146
Westall, Robert 50
white lines 101
Whiteread, Rachel 62
window 36
Wolfe, Maxine 4
womb 2, 111, 118
Wright, Alexis 78

YouTube 43, 130

'As a final bit of evidence for the superordinacy of the concept of place over the idea of land, let me submit the Irish word for land itself: the word is "farran", but it used to be written "fearann", which translates literally as "man there".'

Donna Birdwell-Pheasant – 'The Home "Place": Center and Periphery in Irish House and Family Systems', in Birdwell-Pheasant and Lawrence Zúñiga eds. – *House Life: Space, Place and Family in Europe*, 1999.